DANNY
O'DONOGHUE

THE BIOGRAPHY

DANNY
O'DONOGHUE

THE BIOGRAPHY

David O'Dornan

JOHN BLAKE

Published by John Blake Publishing Ltd,
3 Bramber Court, 2 Bramber Road,
London W14 9PB, England

www.johnblakepublishing.co.uk

www.facebook.com/Johnblakepub facebook.
twitter.com/johnblakepub twitter

First published in paperback in 2014

ISBN: 978-1-78219-762-1

British Library Cataloguing-in-Publication Data:

A catalogue record for this book is available from the British Library.

Design by www.envydesign.co.uk

Printed in Great Britain by CPI Group (UK) Ltd

1 3 5 7 9 10 8 6 4 2

The right of ... to be identified as the author of this
work has ... by him in accordance with the Copyright,
Designs and Patents Act 1988.

Papers used by John Blake Publishing are natural, recyclable
produ... made from wood grown in sustainable forests.
... ses conform to the
env ... ... regulations of the country of origin.

This book is dedicated to Lexi
and Charlie, my two little rock stars.

ACKNOWLEDGEMENTS

Thanks to all my family and friends for their love and support, but especially to my wife Tara, who was left to run a house and raise our children almost single-handedly while she allowed me the time to work on this book at home.

Special thanks again to Rosie Virgo from John Blake Publishing for having the faith in me to approach me for a second book, and her great encouragement and kind words throughout the process. I must be doing something right.

Warm thanks too to the following people who I spoke to about Danny: Ralph McLean, Andrea Begley, Nikki Hayes, Shane Lynch and Connor Phillips, and also to my employers Independent News & Media for picture assistance.

And to 'The Script Family' and fans of Danny

O'Donoghue who have bought this book, I hope you enjoy reading it. My family and I thank you from the bottom of our hearts.

David O'Dornan, 2014

CONTENTS

CHAPTER 1

BORN TO BE
A ROCK STAR

Music really was written in The Script for Danny O'Donoghue – it was in his blood. Daniel John Mark Luke O'Donoghue came into the world on 3 October 1980, the sixth and last child to Ailish and Shay O'Donoghue, who was a professional musician and a member of the successful Irish showband The Dreams.

'Music was in the family,' says Danny. 'My dad was a piano player and my brothers were all in bands. Dad was a great singer. I grew up in a house full of music.

'We found self-expression through music. Whenever anyone picked on me when I was young I'd go into a room and sing my arse off to deal with the aggression. It was just a way of getting things out.'

His mum Ailish was also an accomplished dancer, but it was his dad's reputation and talent as a musician that really stoked the fires for Danny as a kid. He would spend hours bashing away on the keys, encouraged by his father. That encouragement and enjoyment would develop into learning the instrument properly and laying an early foundation for his future success.

So good had Shay been in his pomp that he played with legends like Roy Orbison and Tom Jones – later to stand shoulder to shoulder with Danny on the hit TV talent series *The Voice*. 'Tom remembered him,' Danny explained to the *Sun*, recalling one incident when Shay, who acted as driver for Tom when the Welshman came to Dublin, took him out to the seaside at Dun Laoghaire. 'Me dad dropped him off to go swimming and was waiting. Tom came back to the car and Dad was like, "Where are your shoes, Tom?" and Tom was like "Someone stole them!" Someone had seen Tom Jones getting in and nicked his bloody shoes.'

With anecdotes like that, it's clear Danny's was no ordinary upbringing. Anything could happen in the O'Donoghue household depending on which heady mix of rock stars happened to be around at the time to jam together and party.

'Growing up I used to sleep in a place called the music room and there was a mattress on the ground and a piano in the corner,' Danny told *The Independent*. 'Friday, Saturday, Sunday it was party time in our house. I remember my dad told me a story about he and my mum waking up and Phil Lynott from Thin Lizzy was in the bath. They didn't know if he was dead. They'd been having a session playing.'

Growing up in that environment, Danny could see early on the impact the life of a musician had on a family. 'They were all singers and dancers with big personalities,' he told *The Observer*. 'You had to find yourself among that – it was quite hard. I'd seen how much Mum missed my dad and my brothers when they were on the road touring.'

It was because his dad and brothers were away from home so often that Danny didn't pick up the guitar until he was 14. 'I ran the other way,' he says. 'I'd say, "I'm never going to leave you, Mum." I wanted to be an artist. I was drawing morning, noon and night.'

Being the youngest child meant that Danny had to get used to standing up for himself, fighting for attention in the busy O'Donoghue household. 'Yeah, you do become Paddy Last,' he says. 'You're last at the table, you get everybody's hand-me-downs.'

But thanks to his dad and his brothers, Danny had access to a broad range of music as a child that would help influence and shape his direction as an artist later in life. 'I grew up listening to James Taylor but my brothers were into Metallica and The Police, and of course my dad was a pianist with Tom Jones and Roy Orbison,' he says. 'We had all those records in the house. It's a cliché but Stevie Wonder was an early inspiration – his ability to go up and down the scales amazed me.'

Music coursed through his veins thanks to his upbringing, but Danny believes it was the songs he grew up with as much as his DNA that contributed to his powerful voice. In fact, Danny was so captivated by genres such as Motown, soul and R&B in his formative years that they would play an important role throughout his career. 'When I was growing up I didn't want to be a musician – I wanted to be black,' he says. 'I grew up trying to emulate a singer like Conner Reeves, who isn't well known outside Ireland, because he was a white guy who sounded like a black guy.'

His dad had rubbed shoulders with mainstream pop stars and composed music as well as playing – it was easy to see how Danny would be inspired to follow in his footsteps. He looked up to his big brother Dara too, who played in folk rock group The Big Geraniums, who formed in 1990, had some success landing a record deal and are still going today. 'We were all in bands at one point,' he says. 'We were all on *The Late Late Show* in different bands over the years.'

Danny was raised in the south Dublin suburb of Ballinteer, where he would spend many a day in nearby Marlay Park. 'It's where I used to go drinking with the lads when I was younger, and it's where I learned to ride a bike.' It was there, too, that he had his first kiss, with a girl at school. 'I was about nine,' he recalls of that innocent moment behind Whitechurch Parish Church. Little did he know that he would one day return to Marley Park with The Script to play for thousands of fans, supporting Alanis Morisette and Lenny Kravitz in 2008.

The first record Danny ever bought was The Monkees'

'Daydream Believer'. 'Me and my brother bought that and an A-ha album at the same time. I loved The Monkees' TV show. It reminded me of my family – four guys jumping about playing instruments.'

Another early influence was an old seven-inch vinyl record of The Beatles' 1966 hit 'Paperback Writer'. 'This was the first one I played because the riff in the verse really got me going. I must have been about eight years old at the time.' Later Danny's musical life would come full circle when The Script supported the man who co-wrote it, Paul McCartney, on tour in the US.

Danny hadn't even hit his teens when he first tried his hand at songwriting – and had the guts to have a stab at performing it live as well. 'I was 12 and it was called "I Want To Be With You",' he told *Metro*. 'It was pretty basic stuff. I ended up performing it with my sister at an open mic night in Dublin. It was a full house and I was up there with my polo neck on. It was like: "Holy shit, I love being on stage – this is really cool." It felt like I was having an out-of-body experience and I went cross-eyed staring at the microphone but I knew I wanted to do it again.'

Around the same age he was developing another passion that would become a lifelong love affair – Manchester United Football Club. 'I've been a United fan all my life,' he told the *Sun*. 'I grew up in a United household and my brothers loved the Devils. My dad was a Forest fan but he had to experience some winning so I guess he made me a Man United fan!

'I was quite a late bloomer actually going to see United, but I went to see Liverpool when I was 12. My dad knew one of club directors at Liverpool and for my birthday he asked if I wanted to go and see the team play – it was Spurs v Liverpool. We were in the Anfield boardroom, sitting there in the enemy's belly. I had dinner with all the players and my dad told me, "We're in here now and you have to put the jersey on." So there I was holding the FA Cup wearing a Liverpool shirt. It was the most shameful photo I've ever had!'

Danny's love of football extended to playing the game too. 'I was a goalkeeper for a team in Dublin for about four years. I played schoolboys as well and that was pretty much it. When we started we were supposed to be in the B league, but they had entered us into the A league instead, so we spent a whole season losing every game. We were the exact opposite of Arsène Wenger's Invincibles – the Fucking Disgracefuls!'

Danny was never academic at school – in fact, he even failed his Junior Certificate exams in music. He was a bit of a 'messer' – a joker – in class, and preferred amusing his friends by sticking recorders up his nostrils to play 'When the Saints Go Marching In' than taking things seriously. 'I didn't pay any attention at school,' he told *The Times*. 'I was too busy writing songs. The English teacher called my mother in. I thought I was going to get a bollocking but all she wanted to do was tell my mother how talented I was.'

In the end he dropped out of school before finishing

his Leaving Certificate – in truth, he wasn't interested in education. Only one thing consumed him – song-writing. 'I idolised my dad,' he told *The Observer*. 'I would always bring my songs home to him like a pay cheque. We'd talk about it, the chorus or whatever, and he was really encouraging. My mum now says my dad swore he knew all of this was going to happen ... He had blind faith.'

But later Danny would admit that one of his biggest regrets was 'not learning to read music. I'm self-taught and I play everything by ear.' Despite that, after school he enrolled for the performing arts academy in the Dublin's Digges Lane. He was sure that talent would out – that he didn't need qualifications to fall back on. Music and hard work would take him forward. 'Our motto is that if you don't have a safety net, you won't fall back,' says Danny.

As he got older Danny would get his first taste of festivals as a starry-eyed teenager at the Féile musical festival, then Ireland's biggest music event – held initially in Thurles, Co Tipperary. 'I was a Féile boy – I went to the Trip to Tipp,' he told the *Irish Mirror* in 2011. 'I went on tour with The Big Geraniums and The Frames years ago when I was only a chisseller [Dublin slang for child]. I got the chance to watch The Big Geraniums from the side of the stage at Féile. I'll never forget it – it was 6pm and the band went on and killed the place. So I'm well versed in music festivals. I've been buying festival tickets for years, sneaking in for more.'

As a teen, Danny was drawn to chart-friendly sounds, especially the smooth R&B of acts such as Boyz II Men and TLC and the producer Babyface. His future friend for life and band mate in The Script, Mark Sheehan, was of like mind. 'They were colourful, everyone was dancing, there were incredible harmonies and it looked like great fun,' he told *The Sunday Times*, 'as opposed to looking at your shoes, playing slit-your-wrists music, which I was then getting from all angles.'

Mark, who grew up in the rough and tumble inner-city area of James's Street in The Liberties, in the shadows of the Guinness brewery, is convinced their lives would have taken a very different turn had they not found music. He knows too well that many people he knocked about with when he was younger fell into a life of crime. 'I never went hungry,' says Mark, 'but I fought every day of my life. Back then the only way to express yourself was to rob cars, or write on the walls.'

Their roots would ensure there was never any danger that they would get big heads when fame arrived. 'We take all this celebrity stuff with a pinch of salt,' Mark says.

He told the *Irish Sun* more about his gritty upbringing: 'It sounds like a cliché but music did save us in many ways. It certainly changed my life. I was a late bloomer when it came to music. I didn't start getting involved until I was about 15 and up until that point in my life I was doing a lot of stupid things.

'Where we grew up was a shithole, I won't romanticise it. It was all stealing cars and getting in trouble, the usual bollocks. Thank God none of us got into serious shit, but it could just have easily gone that way. Music really helped me move away from that life, it gave me a sense that I could break away. That was my way out. But I know people who really took a wrong turn and I'm very conscious of how different things could be for me, and for that reason I'm always so grateful for how things have worked out.'

Strong words from Mark and he would take some flak for them, but he was unforgiving when asked again about their roots by the *Northern Echo*.

'I got a lot of shit for that,' he said. 'But they [his critics] didn't grow up there when I did. 'Did I steal cars? Yes I did. Was I caught up in drugs? Yes I fucking was. Was I in fights every day? Yes I was. Was the area practically derelict? Yes it was. They call that paradise, I call that a shithole.'

For Danny, music meant that his life was a bit different. 'I spent a lot of my childhood singing when the other kids were outside playing football and getting into trouble.'

The pair of them would help keep each other out of trouble when they met for the first time as teenagers in 1994, which marked Danny's first beginnings as a musician proper. They met as strangers but the pair of them soon realised they shared the same tastes as they began messing about and jamming in a shed at the back of Mark's house.

Mark had advertised studio equipment, a four-track

recorder and keyboard he no longer used, in Dublin's *Buy and Sell* magazine and Danny arrived at his door interested in buying the gear. As Danny tested the equipment out, Mark saw his obvious talent. 'I realised he could sing,' he says. 'Also, he could do what I couldn't do.'

It was the big-bang moment that led to Danny and Mark writing music, which Mark would produce. The pair of them would meet almost every day in that shed, consumed with pooling their talents to make music and dreaming of becoming big pop stars. 'Other kids were out there playing football or robbing cars,' says Danny, 'but we were just in there, trying to figure out how these songs were built.'

They were not drawn to typical Irish rock and folk influences, but instead shared an obsession with black artists, from Motown and soul music to American hip hop and R&B. 'Soul is not a black thing or a white thing, it's a human thing,' Mark told the *Coventry Evening Telegraph*. 'When I was a teenager, MTV only came on in Dublin after midnight – it was the fuzzy channel, and for my generation black culture was just a wave through us all. It wasn't about gangs and guns; it was fashion and fun, singing and dancing.'

'Irish people have got soul,' agreed Danny. 'It comes from generations of pain, and generations of under-standing emotion to be able to physically get that in a solid sound. One day I heard Stevie Wonder singing and the hairs on the back of my neck went up. I didn't even know people could sing like that – I'd never heard the acrobatics of it before.'

Throughout his teenage years Danny would spend hours on end, day after day, trying to perfect a similar singing style. 'I'd try and emulate all those records, even down to string arrangements. Some of the best singers have emulated a musical instrument – Amy Winehouse is a saxophone – but the violin is the one for me, the vibrato, you can bring so much heartfelt emotion in.'

'There is something about the way a voice encapsulates a person,' adds Mark. 'The way Danny sings, the raw emotion, when you hear it in front of you, you cannot deny the power.'

Danny would tell the *Irish Times* in 2012, 'That shed was where we first got talking and realised we had a lot in common about what we wanted to do musically. I think of that first meeting in The Liberties whenever I meet one of my heroes – and at this stage I've been privileged enough to meet my entire record collection. There's been times at shows when I look out and the front row looks like my iTunes page!'

'I was always messing around with music since I was a kid,' Mark told the same newspaper in 2008. 'I had these keyboards and would practise away in this little shed in The Liberties. But I always knew that the musical ideas I had in my head wouldn't sound quite right if they came out of my own mouth.

'Just by coincidence, one day I advertised that I was selling some musical equipment – I was 16 at the time –

and this 14-year-old kid came to have a look at it. He was telling me how he was a singer and all of that, so we started messing around with songs together. Now he's the lead vocalist in The Script.'

CHAPTER 2

MY KIND
OF TOWN

Danny and Mark clicked right away. They fast became friends, and barely a couple of months after they'd met they began writing songs together. Instead of buying that music equipment, Danny pooled his resources with Mark's and they started using the gear together.

But pop music wasn't yet making Danny enough to live on, so he had to earn a wage by grafting on a building site, mixing cement. 'That was a tough way to earn a living,' he says now. 'This is easy!' It would be two years before he and Mark would start to piece together a band, after they got together with Paul Walker and Terry Daly at the now defunct Digges Lane performing arts school in Dublin, where Mark was a professional dance instructor in choreography and hip hop dancing.

'There was a great atmosphere,' Paul remembers. 'We

were singing, dancing and auditioning all the time. Boyzone were rehearsing in Digges Lane and Mark was teaching dance routines to B*witched and OTT.' The actor Colin Farrell and Irish dancer Michael Flatley were also clients of Mark.

Mark had met Paul, who had showbiz experience from acting in Irish TV shows and films, to discuss plans to put together a boy band. They wanted the right blend of musicians as members and recruited graphic design student Terry alongside Danny, who was 16 at the time. They decided upon the name Mytown for their group, taking their inspiration from the moment when all four were sitting on a Dublin rooftop looking out over their town.

'I vowed I'd never leave my ma because she always had me pegged as a musician,' Danny told the *Daily Mirror*. 'But then puberty hit and I met Mark. He was teaching at a performing arts school and I joined his class. My mam would say, "You look after him" and he's kept me in line over the years.'

But first Danny took on a side project that, it could be argued, was his first proper stab at pop stardom. A year later, in 1997, as a fresh-faced 17-year-old eager to muscle into a market where the likes of Boyzone and Take That were enjoying success, he was one third of a pop trio called Upfront. With 18-year-olds Ian Colgan and Mark Henderson, they had formed a year previously, when Ian's mum had needed singers for a convention she was arranging. 'It snowballed after that and we did lots of charity shows,' Danny told the *Irish*

Mirror. 'Then Brian and Barry spotted us and offered to manage the group.'

Brian and Barry were the management team of Brian Molloy and Barry Gaster, who counted The Corrs as one of his clients. They took the trio on and by March that year, Danny and Co were aiming for Boyzone's crown, though with a different slant. 'We're more hip hop than pop,' Danny said. 'We're trying to steer clear of the usual four or five-piece boy band thing.'

The group boasted that they were all accomplished singers and dancers, and that Danny was studying piano at the Parnell School of Music at the time. 'We write and sing all our own material,' Mark Henderson said. 'We're sure it will do well.'

Unfortunately it didn't, but that didn't dampen the enthusiasm of Danny, who returned to the fold with Mark and the Mytown boys more eager than ever to make it. Unable to secure a record deal, they turned the shed at the back of Mark's house into a studio (which they call the Madhouse) and started writing and recording songs. As they began to develop a fan base, they released their own single, 'Do It Like This'.

'We put it together ourselves,' Paul said. 'We decided to take a chance and financed it ourselves. It was a good way to get ourselves known and to get a record deal.'

Their big break came thanks to a huge leap of faith from their manager, Eamon Maguire, who raised the cash to fly them to Las Vegas for a showcase gig. 'There were 140 bands performing at the show,' Paul told the

Irish Sun at the time. 'It was all very strange and intimidating. Our manager Eamon Maguire took a huge gamble on us by re-mortgaging his house. But he really believed in us. We actually couldn't get arrested in Ireland – we had to go away to make it. It was hard for us to get a deal as a boy band because we wanted complete control.'

At the show the group did an acoustic set for Universal Music CEO Doug Morris, which was an unnerving experience. 'We've played to huge crowds before but we were never as nervous as that day in front of seven people,' says Danny.

But the gamble paid off and Mytown caused a sensation in the Irish pop music scene by winning a record-breaking IR£15million (Irish pounds) deal with Universal, even though they were complete unknowns and had once been told by Boyzone manager and *X Factor* judge Louis Walsh that they were too ugly to become a top boy band.

But the big investment from Universal meant the heat was on Mytown to produce results quickly, particularly with their debut album. 'The pressure was enormous,' Mark later told *The Sunday Times* in 2009. 'I remember going through Dublin airport and seeing a rolling news ticker and it had something about an Irish boy band signing a record-breaking deal. I was like, "Oh man, we're really setting ourselves up here."'

Paul told the *Irish Sun*: 'We do feel under pressure, but we're very confident it will be a great album. It's hard work but a lot of the songs come easy to us. We wrote 35 and cut it down to 14.'

The band had an unlikely early cheerleader in the form of a Royal – Sarah Ferguson, the Duchess of York. Fergie had stayed in touch with them ever since she'd seen them performing two years earlier. 'She's a lovely woman,' Paul said, 'She's helped us a lot. She was patron of a children's charity we performed for and took us all out to dinner.'

The connection even led to an unlikely gig – in war-torn Bosnia. 'We were asked to go there in the Duchess of York's [Sarah Ferguson's] place,' said Mark, but it wasn't a particularly successful occasion.

'When we performed there, they couldn't express their emotions,' Danny told the *Malay Mail*.

'They just didn't understand that kind of thing,' added Mark.

The fledging boy band were shipped out to the US to launch their bid for pop stardom. 'The reason we initially got out of Ireland was the amount of other talent trying to make it,' Danny told *The Times*. 'You throw a pound in Ireland, you're gonna hit a musician. Or you'll have ten musicians fighting over it!'

On top of that, Danny and Mark desperately wanted to produce music in a similar vein to the big-selling American R&B artists they admired, such as Boyz II Men, and there wouldn't be much scope or appreciation for that if they stayed in Ireland. As Danny put it: 'In Dublin, if you weren't playing the Irish card – if you didn't have a fiddle, or if you weren't like The Corrs – you didn't get a look-in.'

As part of the early promotion trail, Universal pushed the guys all over North America to raise their profile. Initially the move was a great success, with Mytown making it to number one in the Canadian music video charts with the single 'Party All Night'. The track put them ahead of established big name artists like 'N Sync, The Backstreet Boys, Christina Aguilera, Five and S Club 7 in the Canadian YTV charts.

Overall, the fledgling band spent a year across the pond and got another boost when they performed at Nickelodeon's *Big Help* concert in LA. The head of Nickelodeon was so impressed that he insisted their track 'Lifetime Affair' be on the soundtrack of the Nickelodeon movie *Snow Day*. The following year they returned to the US, where they performed at places like Planet Hollywood at Walt Disney World in Orlando.

On 23 May 2000 their self-titled debut album was released in the States and in Australia, but not in Britain or Ireland. Danny and the boys co-wrote many of the songs on it, collaborating with such heavy-hitters as BLACKstreet's Teddy Riley, members of Boyz II Men, and Narada Michael Walden, who had written for Mariah Carey and Whitney Houston.

'We had produced our own demos,' Danny said of a lack of release for the record in Ireland and Britain, 'but the label thought Teddy Riley and Dallas Austin could polish our sound. Our songs were soulful hip hop, or so we thought. In the end, the album never came out. In the States, they said we were too pop. Over here, we were told we were too R&B.'

Terry Daly described the album as 'a variation of romantic ballads, midtempo grooves, and fast street songs'. The album's first single, the dance track 'Body Bumpin'', was produced by Riley, while Wanya Morris, of Boyz II Men fame, co-wrote and produced 'Lifetime Affair'. Thirteen US radio stations picked up the single, including WXXL 106.7 FM, based in Orlando. 'They put on a good performance,' said Pete de Graaff, assistant program director and music director of the Florida radio station. 'Lyrically, they're real good.'

Elsewhere the group collaborated with another member of Boyz II Men, Shawn Stockman, who produced 'The Day' written by Danny, and with Teddy Riley on 'C'mon Everybody' and the remake of the 1980s Wham! classic 'Everything She Wants'. Not least, 'Girl in Tears' was co-written by Billy Steinberg, who wrote Madonna's 'Like a Virgin'.

The promotion drive continued with appearances on *Donny & Marie* and the Nickelodeon programmes *Big Help* and *Snick House*, while a half-hour Nickelodeon special was televised around the time of the album's release. The band also continued to move around the US to try and build their fan base, performing free gigs in places like big malls.

Things got even better when the band were booked to open for Christina Aguilera's *Psychoblast* tour in Canada that July. Even though they never got to meet the headliner herself, the experience was certainly different from anything they'd encountered before. Danny told the *Malay Mail*: 'We spent three weeks touring and on the second night, as we were asleep in our bunks, the driver shouts, "We just killed a moose!" We had to stop and call the police and they came and did the humane thing.

'As far as the tour went, we didn't have time for sound checks, and each show gradually got better.'

'It was a moving experience as "Party All Night" was No 1 in their video charts for six weeks and the fans knew our songs,' added Mark.

The band barely had time to catch their breath before they were flown to Australia to plug 'Party All Night' as their first single there. 'The US is a tough nut to crack,' Terry told *The West Australian*. 'We've stiff competition from bands like 'N Sync and Backstreet Boys but thankfully they do embrace new acts like us. It just takes the time. It's early days still and our album has just come out there.

'We can't control what people think of us. People pick up the single and see four pretty boys on the cover and put it aside. The most important thing is that people give us a chance to learn what we are all about. I really want to bring out the fact that we can play. Everything has been a natural progression rather than a planned, "Let's play it like this."

'When we tried to get signed in the UK, there were so many boy bands, the fact that we played instruments didn't seem to make any difference. But we took our time and said we weren't going to sign a crap deal just to get one. We spent time rehearsing and getting it together to make it perfect. It took a long time to get signed because we did everything ourselves right down to writing the album.

'We have control and we are not in a rush to make ourselves known at the expense of other things. We don't care how other bands are going around doing it.'

A month later it was on to Malaysia to drum up support there and they went down well. 'Our influences may be from the States but we are growing musicians and, as growing artistes, our inspirations will change. It changes constantly,' Mark told the *Malay Mail*. 'We're a boy band but more on the positive side. We sing live on any occasion and we're more involved in this thing than you think.'

'We still hope to be around in 10 years,' Paul told the paper, blissfully unaware they wouldn't last another one. But his optimism was not misplaced and if nothing else, Danny and Mark were gaining valuable experience of the music industry.

'The States was the thing, getting the respect from everybody we worked with,' Mark told the paper. 'But we are the little fish among the big fish. But as little fish, we can create little waves. Hopefully, we'll make it but we're not too worried. We just want to make good music. The States is radio-driven and if you don't get on radio, you can just forget it.'

'If people don't call to ask for your song, that's it,' agreed Danny.

'We don't want to sell ourselves as being Irish,' Mark maintained. 'We want to sell good songs. Coming from a strong Irish musical tradition, it is tough to live up to. We are slightly left field in Ireland. We don't know if it's going to go down well.'

After a short break back home, they returned to Australasia in November and December 2000 for another promotional push. As far as they were concerned they were already working on new material and had 20 songs penned already.

'Right now, we are concentrating on recording our second album,' Danny told the *Sun Daily* newspaper in Malaysia. 'Our record company feels that we should use the free time we now have to start recording a second album because once the first album takes off, we won't have the time [to do it]. What finally gets into the album is another thing but we hope to have as many of our own songs chosen as possible.'

The boys were happy with the ways things had gone for them in the US and the way they had been accepted in Asia. 'Unlike Westlife, who have a fan base of those age between four to sixteen, we do have that age bracket as well as an older bracket like their parents,' said Danny. 'In that way, we are not only going for an older crowd but are actually getting them.'

For Mytown's second album, Danny said they were hoping to go with the same producer for all their songs:

'This is to ensure that each song is linked and have a story to tell.'

He also admitted that he was beginning to love the life of an international pop star. 'I am only 20 and have been to so many countries,' he said. 'You also get to do shows in front of many different people and share in their cultures.'

But while Mytown enjoyed moderate success, they had failed to set the world alight and that was not enough for their mighty record label. 'With the Universal Records thing it was for something like seven albums, but we were only kids and like everyone else were prepared to try anything to make it,' Danny told the *Northern Echo*. 'And there was a lot of hype surrounding us. But if you have a song out and it doesn't work, then bang you're dropped. All the hype in the world can still end in heartbreak.'

But at least Danny had gained valuable experience. He and Mark had been able to write and produce their own songs, and had made vital contacts – and just as importantly had developed a true friendship with Mark.

Looking back on his Mytown days, Danny said his only regret is the polished boy band image he had adopted. 'I look back and cringe at that period,' he told the *Sun* in 2010, 'but without the struggles we wouldn't be where we are today. There is no point in denying your past. I regret the state of my hair and clothes then – it's like looking back at old family photos. But as I travel and meet more fans I realise people don't care.

'I'm not ashamed of that time. I thought I was as cool

as shit. We had a couple of songs we wrote with Teddy Riley from BLACKstreet and we wrote a couple of songs with Boyz II Men, but I'm not ashamed of it as we learned a lot.'

'When you're that young and you get a record deal you think "I'm set for life",' he told the *Herald-Sun*. 'But you soon realise, no, you're set for maybe a year and then you're on your own. If anything the failure of it taught us not to take everything for granted. It made us learn about longevity in this business.'

Although it didn't feel like it at the time, Mytown's failure was a blessing in disguise. Had they succeeded, they believe now that they wouldn't have been mature enough to handle fame. 'We wouldn't have been ready for success ten years ago,' Mark said. 'We would have pissed it up the wall.' As it was, the blow of failure meant that they could experience the lows and appreciate the ruthless nature of the music industry. They would learn from their mistakes and handle it differently – and appreciate it more – second time around, should they be so lucky.

'I learned to take nothing for granted after that disappointment,' Mark told *VNU Entertainment Newswire*. 'We were being built up, but it didn't happen. What I took from it was that you have to be aware of the commercial side of things. What I've learned is to take nothing for granted and always keep your business head on.'

'We thought we were The Backstreet Boys or Boyz II Men,' laughed Danny to the *Irish Mirror* in 2011. 'It's only when you look back that you realise, "I was in a boy band." I guess what I learned from that time was how not to dress. But it was great – four lads getting to tour the world. I don't think there's any guy who wouldn't be into that amount of girls screaming when you are 18 or 19.'

The anthemic Celtic soul rock they write now is a different world to the easy-cheesy pop on which they cut their teeth. 'I don't miss anything from those days,' says Danny. 'Mytown fans were young and they were just having fun. Now it's all about the music and the fact that we are a live band. It's a totally different experience.'

'I remember getting that record contract and thinking this was it – I was set for life,' he told *Fabulous* in 2012. 'I was telling my family we're going to make it. And when we didn't it was crushing. But it taught me a lesson and turned me into the person I am today. When The Script got signed, we put the money into a bank account and paid ourselves a wage. I don't know where or when this is going to end.'

CHAPTER 3

THE AMERICAN DREAM

The Mytown adventure was over. Universal had thrown a lot of money at them and jetted them all over the world. True, they had enjoyed some success but it had not been as lucrative as the money men demanded. But Danny and Mark were not ready to call it a day.

The pair had had a taste of the music business and wanted more, but they were unsure of their next move – until they got some sage advice from one of the biggest names in management. 'Through a friend of a friend we got to meet Paul McGuinness [of U2],' Mark told the *Irish Times*. 'Myself and Danny went into his office and played some of our stuff on acoustic guitars for him. He was very helpful. He pointed us towards a few publishing companies in the US, and eventually we got this publishing deal over there which allowed us to develop as songwriters.'

In 2001, Danny and Mark, still licking their wounds, headed to America. Having arrived with just £125 in their pockets, they managed to carve out a living there for the next few years. 'I was always being told to get a proper job by numerous girlfriends, mates, family, everyone,' says Danny. 'They all thought I was mad. But you keep it in your head that this is a dream and hopefully some day it'll work out.'

Danny and Mark moved first to Orlando in Florida before settling in Los Angeles, but they weren't quite stepping into the unknown. Thanks to their Mytown experience they had lived in the States for a year and amassed quite a few contacts. Key amongst them was Teddy Riley, who had co-written and produced Mytown's first single, 'Body Bumpin''. These days Grammy award-winning Riley is said to be worth in excess of $80 million, having produced for the likes of Michael Jackson, Usher and Bobby Brown.

Thanks to knowing Riley – and the fact that the boys could boast technical and musical skills – they landed on their feet. They wouldn't have to wait tables or pull pints to pay the bills, but they couldn't simply walk into a job in music. Yes, they had worked with Riley before, but that was as fresh-faced boybanders. He still needed to be convinced they could cut it musically and, thanks to a combination of 'hustling' and Irish charm at his Virginia Beach base, they managed to blag their way inside and an impromptu busking audition won them a gig helping Riley with vocals and work at the studio.

'It was probably the gift of the gab that got us the gig,' Mark told the *Irish Times*. 'Most days, we would be just making the tea, but other days we would be involved in programming or actually playing on a record. A fantastic learning experience for us both. From there, we made a few more contacts and then got some work with The Neptunes. But it was still very hard going and we did really struggle at times.'

'It was real bottom-up stuff – assistant to the tea maker and all of that,' Danny told the same newspaper in 2012. 'I remember once sitting on a couch for three days in a row trying to come up with a top line melody for a big producer. If you left that couch someone else would take your place. All those broke years in the US were like what that book [Malcolm Gladwell's *Outliers: The Story of Success*] says about having to put in the 10,000 hours work at something before you can be successful at it.'

As studio hands, Danny and Mark were providing songs, remixes and production for the kind of R&B figures they had once idolised. 'These people were making great livings and getting to be musically expressive through songwriting and production,' says Danny.

It wasn't as glamorous as it might sound though, says Mark. 'LA is the hardest place to surface in. Everyone is following some sort of dream. Out of all the struggle there, the silver lining was working with Class A producers like Teddy Riley and Rodney Jerkins: they had so much to offer.'

Mark and Danny even built a mini-studio in their flat

in the Venice Beach district of LA – echoes of their 'Madhouse' studio at the back of Mark's house in Dublin – where they could continue to hone their skills outside their professional work. From working with the likes of Dallas Austin and The Neptunes, the boys started to build their reputation – and ended up writing and producing songs for some of the biggest stars in the pop world, such as Justin Timberlake, Britney Spears, Boyz II Men and TLC. 'It was an amazing thing to do,' says Danny. 'I was young and writing and producing for Britney Spears and TLC. When the times were good, it was great, but we were really penniless for most of the time we were there.'

Danny was so skint he was walking around in a pair of shoes with holes in their soles, but that didn't stop him from trying to look the part. In a bid to make the right impression as he rocked up to a meeting with big-time players in the music scene, he got a mate who owned a flash car to take him to the door. He had also borrowed a Rolex to sparkle on his wrist – it was broken, but who was to know? He'd take the risk that no one would ask him the time. 'It was really hard,' he says. 'Ask anyone who goes to LA with no money.'

But Danny and Mark had grown up in a part of Dublin where people have to fight for everything they have. 'Mark and I were little wheeler-dealers, like Del Boy and Rodney,' Danny told *The Observer*. 'I was Rodney, the plonker. We'd remix one song for Justin Timberlake and then say, "Oh yeah, we made the whole album." You big yourself up, you make your name.'

The world of R&B in the US is a close-knit circle and it's hard to break in. For two raw, pasty-faced Irish unknowns to make their way into the inner sanctum was unheard of. But here they were and slowly word spread. They started to become the go-to guys for something fresh and different. One day a stranger in denim turned up at their door. 'He was like, "Yo, you those Irish guys working with Teddy? Check out my tape, I've got some beats if you wanna write some stuff over it,"' Danny recounted to *The Times*. 'It was Pharrell Williams of The Neptunes, and he was giving us a cassette to write on! This was when he was charging three grand for a track. Now he's, like, 200 grand a track! And that tape, it was so far ahead of its time.'

But that was the exception, not the rule. 'There was nothing glamorous about it,' Danny told *The Sunday Times*. 'We'd get a remix in January, and that would pay the bills until March. We had to become jacks of all trades. One day, I'd be on turntables for TLC or remixing Beenie Man, then Mark would do some programming or get a gig playing a guitar part. We were mostly scraping by.'

Danny even had to sleep in their first studio for six months because he had nowhere to live as they tried to eke out a living as producers. 'We were broke,' he told the *Sun*. 'Food was going off in the fridge as the electricity went so we had to rob the ice to keep our food chilled. Sometimes it was off for four or five days until we earned enough money to switch it back on.'

'We were these two Irish guys, running down the street with bags of ice!' he added to *The Observer*. 'We didn't have a pot to piss in but we were smiling the whole way.'

A remix for Justin Timberlake after he left 'N Sync got them hired by Jive to help the label's new pop signings establish their sound, but all the while they were yearning to create music for themselves. 'We always write from our own experience,' says Danny. 'When someone else sang our lyrics, they never came across as we intended.'

Even hanging out with the likes of Timberlake was no guarantee when it came to pulling women, Danny admitted. 'We were in an LA club with Justin and these girls started chatting us up. It was all going great until they wanted to meet Justin. Quick as a flash they were gone ...'

It might not have worked on that occasion, but Danny and Mark's Irish lilt was usually a tried-and-tested pulling technique in the States. 'The accent works a treat abroad,' says Danny. 'When we're in the States we'd go to different ends of a bar and shout: "What are you having? Do you want a Guinness?" All the girls will be like: "Oh, are you from Ireland?" It's a good ice-breaker.' It certainly worked for Mark – he ended up meeting future wife Reena during their time there.

And that was their life for the best part of seven years: it was a grind and took a lot of graft to survive but they were making a name for themselves. They were not just becoming better songwriters and producers but adding extra strings to their bow as programmers, engineers, backing singers and session guitarists, and their contacts book was growing.

'We spent a lot of time in America, studying the charts, getting to know the industry and really studying the place,' says Danny. 'America is unlike anywhere else: there are so many different marketplaces and genres. Production and songwriter-wise, it gave us an inkling into what America would find palatable.'

The pair even blagged their way to Australia at one point to work with R&B dúo Shakaya, writing most of their 2006 album *Are You Ready*, although that one tanked. They also wrote with Aussies Delta Goodrem, Guy Sebastian, Selwyn and Tammin Sursok.

But this wasn't the life Danny and Mark had imagined for themselves. It was all well and good being the guys behind the guy, but more and more they were itching to go out on their own. They knew they had it in them to be successful recording artists in their own right. 'There was something in me which just wasn't satisfied,' says Danny. 'It's hard when you give your song to another artist and they butcher it.'

They already knew as much as most about how to make a radio-friendly pop song. Now, after more than seven years working for Timberlake, TLC, Britney and The Backstreet Boys, it was time to write a new Script.

CHAPTER 4

THE FIRST CHAPTER FOR THE SCRIPT

D anny is blessed with an incredible voice, self-belief and obvious good looks. In short, he is the perfect front man for a rock band. But most of all he has a natural gift for music. Like his dad before him he's an accomplished pianist, and he has the ability to dig deep into his emotions and write great lyrics. Music courses through his veins, whatever his lack of formal education.

Danny had forged a true friendship with Mark and together they had learned the nuts and bolts of the music industry. They had become skilled producers, composers and writers – they knew exactly what it took to be successful and were almost ready to prove it. As well bringing a songwriting ability on a par with Danny's, Mark could play guitar. They just needed some percussion to complete the sound they had developed over the best part of a decade.

Mark was on a visit back to Dublin in 2005 when he came across Glen Power, a session musician they had met through a mutual friend a year earlier. Glen was drumming for cover bands at weekends and spent the rest of his week messing around in his home studio in Stillorgan. The son of a cabaret singer, his influences and tastes in music were primarily stadium-rock bands like U2, The Police and Simple Minds.

Mark immediately thought Glen could be the final piece of the jigsaw, and invited him to Los Angeles. Glen had only intended to spend two weeks there with the lads on a holiday. But instead of partying or catching a few rays, he found himself heading straight from the airport to a jamming session in the studio. Four hours after getting off the plane, The Script was born.

'He is one of the best drummers I've heard but it was a complete accident,' says Mark about the formation of The Script. 'When Dan, Glen and I jammed one day in Venice Beach we stumbled across something.'

Quickly the three of them realised there was a special connection between them.

'We always say production was keeping our lights on, but our lights were really flickering at one point in 2005,' Mark told the *Arizona Republic*. 'We were just writing songs for the sake of writing songs, and I went to a friend of mine, a big producer who had just started his own independent label, Steve Kipner.'

Australian-born songwriter Kipner (Olivia Newton-John's 'Physical', Christina Aguilera's 'Genie in a Bottle') and his business partner Andrew Frampton had their own label Phonogenic, a Sony subsidiary that had broken Natasha Bedingfield.

'I played him the music and he freaked out,' Mark told the *Arizona Republic*. 'He said, "Who is this band?" And I said, "Why?" He said, "Because I'd love to sign them." I said, "It's a band I'm in but we don't have a name yet." I was just broke and we needed to make something work, to be honest.'

The possibility of launching Danny as a solo act was considered, but Kipner and Frampton agreed they would work better better as a band.

'So when I got back to the boys, I said, "They think we're a fucking band and want to sign us," Mark continues. 'And they were all broke at the same time, so they said, "Let's do it." We just came up with the name The Script right there and then.'

The origins of the name lie in the fact that Danny and Mark would call each other up and ask: 'What's the script?' In Dublin a common greeting among friends is 'What's the story?' and 'story' had morphed into 'script' between the pair.

Danny says they chose it because it sounded cool but it has an additional meaning: their songs have full storylines and are like mini-movies. 'They say that two heads are better than one but if you've got three – holy shit!' Danny told the *Nottingham Evening Post* in 2010. 'I like being on a team, that's the best part of it. If you're doing it on your own, you're a singer-songwriter, you've got a guitar and your voice and that's very self-indulgent. In a band, every time you get on stage and play you're coming together with somebody else. I think that's what makes The Script great.'

They still didn't have much cash when they were getting the band off the ground, and initially all they could afford was a studio with no air conditioning.

'We were sweating our arses off,' Mark told the *Express on Sunday*. 'It ended up with me trying to program in my boxers and Danny doing vocals in his.'

'I couldn't get this one part vocally,' Danny added. 'I took my top off and two seconds later I did. Since then it's been a ritual.'

Mark joked: 'I record bottomless. Together, we are a full naked man.'

The boys were gelling and the songwriting was flowing. They were on a roll and it felt like nothing could stop them. The Script had signed a major-label deal without having toured, a rare occurrence in the music industry, but at the same time a massive vote of confidence.

'It was strange,' Mark told the *Irish Times*. 'You know what they always say – "the only time success comes before touring is in the dictionary" – but I think now with the whole Myspace revolution, record labels are having to do things differently and do things like signing a band before they tour.

'New talent has to be developed in new ways these

days. But I think the label knew that we would be able to produce the album ourselves, so that was one hurdle out of the way, and whenever we came back to Dublin, we could always sell out Whelan's [a famous live music bar], so that helped too.'

Yes, they had belief in their ability and a pretty decent CV, but they were still pleasantly surprised to land the deal at this stage of the band's development. 'From the way the three of us look, to all our influences, it means it shouldn't work,' Mark says. 'It sounds like a disaster. We just appeared. No media coverage at all. We're pretty much a faceless band.'

But just when it looked like everything was falling into place tragedy struck – Mark's mum Rachel was hospitalised and it was unclear how long she might live. 'She was the reason we came back to Ireland,' Mark – whose dad Gerard died when he was 14 – told the *Irish Mirror*. 'We signed our record deal in America then moved home to record the album because she had a stroke. She was in hospital for 10 months and that is what brought me back to Dublin.

'The lads came back with me. I have a small studio, more like a shed, at the back of the James's Street house where I grew up. It was right next to the hospital so I was able to go in and do nightshifts with my mum, write lyrics and then come home and write and record more.

'She heard some songs but she didn't get to hear everything. She felt if you were doing a show that people came to watch, then that was a success. She taught me not to gauge my success on money. I know you have to keep the lights on but in general we do everything because of passion and our love for music. So in her eyes I was always successful because I was following my dreams.'

It was gut-wrenching for Mark to see his mother's life wasting away but this was not going to derail The Script's bid to be rock stars before it had started in earnest. It was not what his mum would have wanted her boy to do, and he wanted to make her proud. 'You've got to turn around and move forward,' he says.

Mark poured his heartbreak into his work. 'It was great for me because I had time to spend with my mother which was so important but I also had time to do what I loved and what helped me cope which is make music,' he told the *Irish Sun*. 'When she passed away I was left with a pool of emotion which of course you dig into when you're recording songs. I don't know if going through a tough time can make you a better musician, maybe you're more in tune with your feelings.'

'He was in the hospital with his mother every day, and he'd voice a lot of the stuff that was going on,' adds Danny. 'A lot of it was brilliant. We suddenly hit a curve where we were writing very honestly.'

'I would spend every night at Mum's bedside, writing down how I felt while she slept, then go straight to the studio,' Mark told *The Sunday Times*. 'There were so many emotions rattling round, the songs poured out of us. "We Cry" came from walking down James's Street early in the morning, smelling Guinness from the brewery and watching girls who should have been at school pushing babies in prams.

'We'd walk past girls with babies called Mercedes or Diamond. You can laugh, but the reason these girls give their kids "expensive" names is because they honestly believe they are giving their children a better chance in life. In no way are we looking down on them.'

The band had returned to Dublin to allow Mark to be with his mum – but before long Danny and Glen too would suffer heartbreak and pain. Danny was left devastated when his dad Shay, who he truly adored, died suddenly, and then Glen suffered a severe head injury. On a night out with his parents, the drummer slipped in the bathroom of his local pub in Stillorgan, hitting his head off the sink and then off the ground. Glen's dad Gary urged him to go to the nearby St Vincent's Hospital. 'He saved my life,' Glen told the *Irish Daily Mail* in 2012. 'I wanted to finish my pint, but my dad told me to go.'

Glen was quickly moved to Beaumont Hospital where he underwent an emergency craniotomy, a procedure that involves cutting into the skull to relieve pressure from a bleed on the brain. 'He was read his Last Rites and all,' says Mark. 'They seriously believed he was about to die.'

'I had a fractured skull and it couldn't have happened at a worse time,' Glen continues. 'We were seeing some real success and then bang. I woke up in a hospital bed with 30 staples in my head. I was so scared. I thought that was it and my life was over.

'Then I had the fear over whether or not I could still

drum and whether I had the ability to be a musician. I got out of hospital after nine days and I headed straight to rehearsals to see if I still had what it took. I remember the first day I played and it wasn't the same. I panicked and thought: "This isn't it. What am I going to do?" The bang in the head had shaken everything and I actually had to go back and learn everything again. I was really worried.

'Then, one morning, I went in and everything clicked. The slickness came back and I got down on my knees and just started praying. It gave me a newfound appreciation of life and I am even more thankful for what I have, an attitude of gratitude.'

All three of the band channelled their inner strength to use their harsh life experiences in their songwriting. There was no shortage of inspiration and emotional outpourings as they developed their blend of pop-rock Celtic soul and R&B in the shed at the back of Mark's house.

'It had the feel of a pirate radio station,' Mark told *VNU Entertainment Newswire*. 'The Guinness brewery was across the road – we could see the smoke coming from their big chimneys. Coming from where we did, there was a lack of options for young people: You were expected to be a plumber or an electrician ... never a singer or dancer or actor.'

As they got their band off the ground, the boys had high hopes about making their mark in Dublin. They'd been in Mytown, worked with major names in the record industry in the States and had a record deal. They knew Dublin's biggest music impresario Paul McGuinness. And they were three Dubliners themselves. So what could possibly go wrong when they booked the Sugar Club for one of their early gigs?

'It held 200 people,' recalls Danny. 'I thought we might sell quite a few tickets but—'

Just 26 people turned up and most of them were friends and family, yet ever-optimistic Danny played on regardless, not vexed in the slightest by the turn-out. 'I always think everything's going to get better,' he says. 'I'm like that. I'm always moving forward, moving on.'

'Twenty-six people knew me,' he told *The Times* in 2013. 'That's where we were back then. We were actually starving. We went from one thing to another trying to get money together. We couldn't afford to heat our houses and we barely ate. Believe me, I do know about all that but I always thought it would change. I'm a grafter, an optimist. I couldn't believe it wouldn't all turn out good.'

Crucially the band, and Mark in particular, was clever enough to have an eye on marketing and drumming up a fan base. Thanks to the internet, he was building the band's profile, and not just on the standard platforms for musicians like Myspace. One innovative idea was 'Beer O'Clock' – a version of a meet and greet, where they would post the name of a Dublin pub and would join fans for a drink. If they were to try that now they wouldn't be able to find a bar big enough. But back then it was ideas such as that, an 'online tour' of the Madhouse and live broadcasts on the internet that struck a chord with eager music fans.

Myspace is a mainstay for all aspiring bands and The Script were no different. They would spend at least an hour a day replying to messages from fans. It wasn't just about building their profile and enjoying a friendly relationship – there was an added reason to give fans so much access, and it was another genius move. The guys were in effect conducting their own market research: by asking fans for their feedback, the band were able to get a handle on what they were doing right by taking note of which songs the fans liked and which ones they didn't.

'We had blind belief in these songs,' says Danny. 'We were seeing how people reacted to them, which just spurred us on.'

'Living in LA helped us understand the music culture and craft our own style,' Mark told the *Irish News of the World*. 'We were in boardroom meetings in record firms where we got to hear what labels look for in their acts. Our sound focuses on versatility. We've more freedom because we don't fit into any one genre.'

Danny agreed: 'Being there had an amazing influence on us. We're the opposite to European music which is all guitars – we're a cross between European and Irish music and American melodies.'

And thanks to their longstanding relationship with U2 guru Paul McGuinness the boys could again get coaching in how to get things right.

'We were invited to Christmas dinner in Dublin with the Edge and U2's management,' says Mark. 'I was able to burn his ear about his recording techniques.'

The excitement was almost all too much for Danny, who skulled so much booze that he embarrassed himself in front of rock royalty. 'Danny was getting more drunk and we were like, "We better get him home" and as he went to sit down there was no actual chair behind him and fell mid-air and went down on his ass,' Mark told the *Geelong Advertiser*. 'If that wasn't bad enough, we excused ourselves from the table and Danny stepped out and fell down a flight of stairs in front of Bono.'

'I fell face down the stairs, pissed out of my head in front of U2,' Danny confessed to the *Irish Sun*. 'They'd invited me to a greyhound race track for Christmas dinner – but I didn't have any dinner. I went straight for the wine and I got really drunk. Then we were leaving to go to a club and I fell down 12 steps right in front of them.'

It wasn't the first time drink had got Danny into trouble, either. 'I smashed six windows in the downstairs of my ma's house,' revealed Danny. 'I was drunk and I was fighting with my sister. I shut the door and smashed both windows 'cause I slammed it so hard.'

But it's the band's emotionally raw lyrics, based on life experiences such as this, which have really struck a chord with fans. 'We do what we believe Irish bands do best,' says Mark. 'We sing from the heart.' That heartfelt music – and the fact that Danny in particular is a pin-up – has meant that women are the larger percentage of their fanbase.

And on 8 August 2008 – 08.08.08 – the band would launch their debut album and explode onto the scene in style.

CHAPTER 5

TOGETHER
WE CRY

Danny had been left stunned and heartbroken when his dad Shay died suddenly on Valentine's Day, 14 February 2008. 'One day I went to England, saw my dad in the morning and he was fine, then came back and he'd had a heart attack and he was gone.' His father had suffered an abdominal (stomach) aortic aneurysm at the age of 63. It would haunt Danny that his father would not be around to see the heights of his success.

'I came home so that Mark could spend time with his mum – little did I know that I was actually getting to spend that precious time with my dad,' Danny told *The Sunday Times*. 'But then amid all this travesty and disaster, these songs have risen out of it. That was the time when it finally came home to me how important music was to me, because in my darkest moments that's what got me through.'

Danny told *The Observer*: 'He was talking to me in the morning and he was dead by night-time. You don't even have time to say, "That's bullshit." I didn't realise that I was getting precious time with my dad. I'd been away for 10 years. I got to know my father as a man. It was: "I know that he loves me but does he like me?"'

To cope with his loss Danny channelled his anger, frustration, pain – every raw emotion he had – into The Script's music, which became 'a proper fucking punchbag' as a result. 'It got me through,' he told *The Observer*. 'Everything he'd taught me went into the album ... every piece of that pain and hurt. The only justification there is for pain is art ... to make the pain into something totally different. Something that was horrible for you can help somebody else.'

As you would expect with a musical family like the O'Donoghues, practically the entire clan got up to perform at the funeral, a true Irish wake in that sense as they gave their old man a proper send-off. Yet the experience did not bring him closer to God. Danny is a man who is often spiritual without being overtly religious. While he wears his heart in his sleeve and embraces the positive energies around him – or channels the negative energies into his work, turning them into a positive force – his dad's death still made him question his faith.

'I find it hard sometimes, in my deepest, darkest moments, to believe,' he admits. Squinting his eyes, and tilting his head, staring into space as if addressing the man upstairs himself, he adds: 'Really, did you have to take my dad away?'

Danny told the *Irish Mirror* that it was his deepest regret that his dad wasn't alive to see his career really take off with The Script. 'My dad passed away as we were making the album. He meant everything to me and to not have him here to see this is a big regret. Funnily enough, he was the only person in my life that was telling me the whole time this was going to happen. When a lot of other people doubted me, he was the man who said, "Listen kid, it's going to happen."

'It hurts because he didn't know that we got to No 1 in Ireland and England. He would have loved that. He was a musician himself, he performed, managed bands and I know he would have been really chuffed to see one of his own kids go out and do this. He was proud of me since I was a nipper, even when I was a tearaway child.'

In 2012 he would add to *The People* when he was a coach on the TV singing contest *The Voice*, 'He was a massive fan of music. He was always proud of me – he would be proud of what I am doing now.'

Danny is a deeply emotional and spiritual human being. He would poignantly mark his love for his dad and the day of his untimely passing with a big tattoo (he has another which says 'Irish Power') on his left arm – 'It was Valentine's Day. That's why I have a rose tattoo' – but more than that he would channel his pain into his songwriting.

The Script's song 'If You Could See Me Now' from

their album *#3* was written in memory of him – and Mark's late parents – three years later. 'The song is about what he would say to me now if he was here,' says Danny. 'It's my favourite song off the album, without a doubt. On stage when I sing it I do feel my father is looking down on me.'

Danny admitted he needed some Dutch courage before he could pour his feelings out at first. 'Dad taught me that music is a home for your pain,' he says. 'He told me not to keep my feelings inside me, because he knew it'd fuck me up. But I'd been a mess in the studio for three weeks leading up to writing that song.'

Eventually, Mark brought whiskey in to get the song started. 'We each had a couple of glasses and I just started writing,' adds Danny. 'It's tough to sing that one live, but people need to see that it's OK to show that you're hurt.'

CHAPTER 6

THE SCRIPT
ARRIVE

'We wrote this album at a very hard time in our lives,' Mark told *MX* in Australia. 'It was like therapy sessions for me. I was writing lyrics while I was at the hospital with my ma and I felt like I was writing a piece of shit.'

Danny was sharing his pain after losing his dad. It meant the songs on their eponymous debut album would have a searing honesty and raw emotion to them.

'It all hit us at once,' says Mark. At one point it sent their heads spinning so much that The Script almost broke up before the record was finished. 'I was going through a hard time, I thought we weren't going to make it as a band,' Mark confesses. 'I wanted to say "Fuck all this." I remember me ma saying to me, "Every end is also the beginning of something new. You have to look at it this way."'

Their debut album was ready and Danny knew they had stellar tracks in 'We Cry', 'The Man Who Won't Be Moved' and 'Breakeven' that would see them arrive with a bang.

'It was ten years of trying,' he explained to the *Northern Echo* in 2010. 'But after all those years of trying we're just getting it right. I think what we've begun to understand is what it takes to create a great song.

'As a writer you're always trying to write the perfect pop song, and I think that "Breakeven" was the one. It's not one that people pick up on immediately, but after three or four listens we feel it really covers the issues of love and heartbreak or loss.

'The trick is trying to find something that hasn't been said before. Our production skills really kind of came to the fore on that one with the melody and taglines and chorus, added to the skills we'd already learned, produced this song at a special time for us.'

Danny says that the three of them share a common energy that allows them to feel the joys and pains together, feeding off each other when it comes to tragedy or ecstasy. It leaves him super-charged to sing their heartfelt lyrics. 'For me the voice is nothing without great lyrics and a great melody ... and in my opinion you won't find a dud lyric on The Script albums,' he says. 'If it doesn't make the hairs on the back of my neck stand up, then there's nothing going on.'

But all that emotion in their records counts for nothing if he can't channel the same energy into every performance on tour. 'The CD is a moment in time but when you come and see us live, that's when a lot of the things we do make sense,' he says. 'Nine times out of ten, the fans say: "You sound better than you do on CD." I think this comes from the crowd who bring their own energy ready to join in with me on the choruses. It's a big-time family affair.'

Danny would adapt this nickname for their devoted fans as their reputation spread, calling them 'The Script Family'.

When The Script were ready to launch in 2008, the *Daily Star* were ahead of the pack. The first paper to embrace the hot new act, they had reviewed the gig at the Borderline in London that January and said, 'Their debut single isn't out until April but already the buzz around the Irish trio is like a swarm of bees. They're getting solid radio play and the venue was packed to the rafters, though its tiny size did not do much for their polished and intricate sound.

'Singer Danny O'Donoghue's blessed with a soulful R&B-tinged voice – not unlike Maroon 5's Adam Levine – and he used it to dazzling effect in this short-but-sweet set. That forthcoming single "We Cry" is a clear highlight and "Rusty Halo" shows The Script's more upbeat side. But it was "Talk You Down" that really stole the show.'

But a month later the band suffered a setback when their support slot with The Hoosiers was thrown into disarray after Danny, 26 at the time, suffered a collapsed lung. He was devastated to have to cancel a string of shows, including one at home in Dublin.

'I was sitting at home having a sausage sandwich with my sister when I felt this aching pain,' he told the *Daily Star*. 'I went to the hospital and they told me my lung had collapsed. Unlike Howard Donald, it wasn't due to performing. It's simply that tall, skinny men are prone to it.'

Danny eventually got the go-ahead to return to the tour after some rest, but only on the condition that he look after his body. 'I'm not allowed to smoke, drink or play football for three months,' he said, 'but the worst thing was cancelling the Dublin show. Playing at home is always deadly.'

By March the momentum was building. The boys were on Phonogenic Records – part of the RCA Label Group, itself a division of Sony BMG (now Sony Music Entertainment). The Script were now all set to be Sony BMG's first Irish act to launch worldwide simultaneously, with their first album going on sale in July in the UK, Europe and, most impressively, the US, where it was hoped their radio-friendly sound would go down a treat.

'It's mad – we can't get our head around the fact so many people are loving songs I wrote more as a diary to get my emotions out of my head,' said Danny at the time. 'Getting America on board already is mind-blowing.'

Their debut single 'We Cry' was already getting lots of attention ahead of its April release, with BBC Radio 1 and music industry magazine *Record of the Day* backing the band. Danny couldn't believe the reaction. 'The response we're getting to a song we wrote in a crappy shed in Dublin is amazing,' he said. 'People are gravitating towards our lyrics.'

The time spent in America working as producers was to pay off when it came to helping The Script keep up its momentum. Thanks to Danny's friendship with the rapper Kenna, The Script were recommended to Pharrell Williams, which led to a support slot at N*E*R*D's Brixton Academy gig in London. 'Kenna used to stay on my floor in Dublin and he went to school with Pharrell,' says Danny. 'He put in a good word and the next thing we were supporting them in London.'

Danny and Mark were already known to Williams from their time in America – Williams and Chad Hugo were signed by Teddy Riley – and N*E*R*D was a side project of The Neptunes. It ended up a real-life case of friends reunited when N*E*R*D saw them and remembered Mark and Danny had worked with the band on one of their albums in Los Angeles. 'We turned up for the first show and they were going "I cannot believe it's you Irish guys again," so that was great fun being on the same bill as someone we used to work for,' says Mark.

Young women in particular adored The Script – their early Myspace friends were almost entirely female, and an appearance in a Bebo online soap saw them cast as pop-star heartthrobs.

The band soon began to understand what it was like to have dedicated fans – and perhaps some over-dedicated ones. 'There were three girls at a N*E*R*D gig we did with three Manchester United jerseys with our names across the back,' Danny told the *Daily Star*. 'I'm the only one that supports them but it was really kind. I recognised one of them because she had emailed us on Myspace. Then a week later we were in Amsterdam and they were in the front row. That night they give us three brand new PSP hand-held PlayStations. I felt bad so I haven't taken mine out of its packaging yet.'

'He felt bad but me and Mark were like: "Woohoo, thanks very much!"' grinned Glen.

'We Cry' debuted at No 15 in the charts and the band were delighted, even though Danny had to put a lid on celebrations because he was still on the mend from his collapsed lung. 'We're going to celebrate tonight and drink lots of water,' he quipped. 'It's hard when you get a bit of good news – you want to get hammered, but we can't.'

The following month, the boys headed for the BBC's Maida Vale Studios to be interviewed by DJ Simon Mayo and record a concert for Radio 2. They were following in some illustrious footsteps – the same slot had had previously featured the likes of Duffy and Adele. When Danny was asked to describe The Script's sound, he rattled out a cheesy quote about 'a new sort of Celtic soul' from the band's press release, then buried his head in his hands in embarrassment.

'Our only ambition was to get one of our songs on the radio,' Mark told *The Sunday Times*. 'Now, every day, we hear that more stations have playlisted the single, or Yahoo is broadcasting one of our gigs, or Perez Hilton has us on his home page. When we supported The Hoosiers in March, we didn't expect anyone to know who we were, but we had every song sung back at us. It's almost going too well. We're waiting for the bad news now, because none of us believes this can continue.'

On 11 June 2008 the band held a lavish launch party at London's One Marylebone Road. The former church is said to cost £10,000 to hire as a venue, but the band stayed true to their roots, laying on Guinness and steak pies and lamb stew with Guinness and Prosecco cocktails. Radio 2 DJ Chris Evans, no stranger to a pint of Guinness, popped in for the party.

Evans had been a fan from the outset, with Jo Whiley also singing their praises early doors after 'We Cry' was Single of the Week on BBC Radio 2. As a new act they were off to a running start, but their launch party was designed to take them up another level.

The band played a live set of tracks from their debut album, set for release on 8 August, including their second single 'The Man Who Can't Be Moved', due out on 28 July. The timing of the album launch was a bold move by the label, coming in the first week of August, historically an industry holiday time and the lowest-selling week in the music year. As well as plugging the single and album, tickets for the band's UK tour to start on 6 August were set to go on sale the next day.

So there was plenty riding on giving a good

performance and making the right impression in the room full of journalists, including media flown in from Australia and the Far East by Sony BMG. Just like the Guinness cocktails, the boys went down a treat. 'We couldn't believe how amazing the venue looked and how much trouble people went to,' Danny says. 'I said a little prayer to me dad before going on, then a thanks after it went so well.'

Danny also told one tabloid journalist that he and the band were living the dream – and determined to enjoy every minute of being rock stars. 'It's a great life,' he said. 'We're going to ride it 'til the wheels come off.'

Both Radio 1 and Radio 2 were giving The Script airplay. Most of the press were behind them and they were starting to get more profile on TV, thanks to performances and interviews on Channel 4's *T4* and ITV's *This Morning*.

The PR angle accompanying the band's promotion drive was that their 'Celtic soul' sound had been described as 'Timbaland meets U2'. 'At first I didn't like any comparisons,' Mark told the *Sun*. 'But I've realised we have one image of who we are but the listener has another. People do say we sound like a U2-type band remixed by Timbaland. I can see that now.'

Danny added: 'We have strong US R&B roots but coming from Ireland you grow up in a rock climate. It feels like R&B/rock to me.'

The band didn't mind the launch parties and TV and radio appearances – it was having to keep impressing international record label bosses that they found harder. 'We're having to go round the world performing to Sony executives at the moment,' said Danny at the time. 'It's just a few big execs in a room – around four or five people. I find those very intimidating. I never can really get into it like I do in front of a crowd.'

From Kelly Osbourne to Peaches Geldof, celebrities were flocking to the band, though Danny had to admit he didn't know who Peaches was when she stopped by his dressing room backstage at the iTunes festival in July 2008.

Such festivals were another way to raise their profile – and get ready for their own tour the following month, taking in cities like Manchester and Liverpool. They played at the daddy of them all – Glastonbury – as well as T in the Park in Scotland and the Party in the Park free concert in Leeds the day before 'The Man Who Can't Be Moved' was released.

'We love performing in front of huge crowds, although we still get really nervous,' Danny told the *Yorkshire Evening Post*. 'Hopefully it'll also be the start of our greatest week so far. Our new single is out and we've got high hopes for it. We just hope the fans like our stuff.'

The fact that their fans lap up their music would be the key to The Script's success – because they wouldn't always win support from the critics, even in their homeland. The *Irish Times* gave 'The Man Who Can't Be Moved' just two stars, but their unkind review did at least concede that it was set to be a hit. 'This is the pop-rock equivalent of one of those god-awful chick flicks one is occasionally forced to sit through on long plane journeys,' they said. 'It's trite. It's unbelievably sappy. And it's likely to be a humongous hit.'

Danny told *Metro* the story behind the song: 'It's about a guy who takes the simple approach to getting back with his ex. He goes back to the street corner where they first met with his sleeping bag and a picture of her and waits for her to turn up again. A crowd forms and news reporters come down. His girlfriend sees him on the news and hopefully, if the sentiment is there, she will come down to see him.'

One man came up to Danny in the street and told him that 'The Man Who Can't Be Moved' had inspired him to get back in touch with his sister, who had been given up for adoption when they were children. 'They found each other again after 25 years,' says Danny. 'And the first thing he handed her was a copy of that song! Those are the people who matter to me.

'I don't care to be the toast of the town, musically. Who cares if you get no-star reviews in the *NME*? Not that we have, by the way.'

Danny's self-assured and confident persona is par for the course for a rock star – it has to be one of the tools of the trade. Yet he doesn't border on arrogant and showed a certain vulnerability – perhaps more modesty rather than self-doubt – when asked by *Metro* when he realised he was any good at singing. 'That's the thing – I still don't think I'm any good at it. The singles have been doing well and I've been getting compliments, which is very humbling. I'm proud I can touch people with my voice.'

Danny told the *Daily Star* that he is in touch with his feminine side, allowing him to express himself more freely through his songwriting. 'Men are scared about showing weakness or emotions, but I've got three sisters so I've never been afraid to show love to people in my life,' he said. 'Growing up with sisters, you see the hurt the male side can give them. It opened up my mind to both worlds, which helped when writing our album.

'Our songs are from therapy sessions. One track called "Breakeven" is about how someone is always left with the lesser piece in life. The worst day for him would be his girlfriend's best day.

'These songs have lifted us through the clouds in life and relationships. It's a great feeling when fans say they relate to them. I've had guys say they gave our song to their girlfriends as it helped them explain what they wanted to say.'

The band's music really struck a chord in Australia. The *Sydney Morning Herald* hailed The Script's 'superlative music' and reserved special praise for their singer. 'Danny O'Donoghue has a sensational soul voice and his bandmates back him to the hilt with a fat R&B sound that owes as much to Van Morrison as it does to Kanye West. The album's first track, "We Cry", is the kind of song you fall in love with, thanks to its sweet melody, killer chorus and O'Donoghue's ageless voice.'

You might think the band would have enough on their

plates with a debut album release, festival dates and a tour, but the guys were still in the market for working with others. They had been consummate networkers throughout their career, so why stop now? It could only help them further their reputation to keep rubbing shoulders with as many stars as possible, so they collaborated with Kelly Rowland on a Stevie Wonder song.

'She approached us saying she loved our music and thought it would be a great idea to collaborate,' says Danny. 'We met and jammed out some ideas and came up with a Stevie Wonder song.' That song was 'Part Time Lover', which they performed together on Channel 4's *T-mobile Transmission* that August, but it was never released as a single.

Another potential collaboration was mooted when the boys met Leona Lewis. 'We were backstage at the MTV Malaysian Music Awards where we had presented an award,' Danny told the *Daily Star*. 'She turned round to us and said, "I'm mad into your music." We were like, "Fucking hell!" because I am like a superfan of hers. I know she came off a reality show and maybe it is not the most admirable thing to do but she is amazing.

'I would love to get into her head a little bit. When we sit down to write with people we really get to know them and their strengths. She is amazing and I think the best is yet to come. I hope we can be the ones to pull it out.'

Thanks to major radio play, 'The Man Who Can't Be Moved' jumped a massive 27 places in one week to hit No 3 in the charts. And on the day of the album launch the boys were back in their native Dublin to perform at HMV in Grafton Street.

The *Irish Times* might have been hard on 'The Man Who Can't Be Moved', but they loved the debut album, giving it four stars. 'Two of the three members of this new Dublin three-piece used to be name producers on the Los Angeles music scene, working with acts such as The Neptunes and Rodney Jerkins,' they wrote. 'They evidently picked up a big bag of sonic tricks along the way: their debut album comes with the sort of studio sheen that other bands take a handful of albums to nail down.

'This is an album that could do serious damage on US radio – it has the sort of sound that radio pluggers are crying out for – and could well establish The Script as fine purveyors of smooth indie soul.'

In answer to the newspaper's observation that their album was 'very un-Irish sounding', Mark said that naturally they were influenced by all the time they had spent in America. 'Obviously, because of our work in the US, the album was always going to have a sort of American sound. I think there's a big difference between American and Irish and British music. It's really all to do with the placement of sounds and how you record them. Contrary to popular opinion, American albums are rawer sounding – typically, they'd use a lot less microphones over the equipment in the studio. Whatever polishing you hear on the final track, is all done in the mixing process.'

Despite that – or maybe because of that – Mark hoped that their music would still strike a chord in the working-class communities where he grew up. 'The kids in The Liberties these days are all listening to 50 Cent, Maroon 5 and Coldplay, but I can hope that they can give us a listen too.'

The Script were on the way up. Fans loved them and were growing in number by the day. Critics too were buying into them and they were getting lots of airplay. And they were making plenty of industry friends along the way into the bargain. But every rock star image needs some rock 'n' roll rivalry and Danny's first run-in came with Radiohead, who didn't see the funny side when he nicked their MTV award in Malaysia for a joke. 'We went to the MTV awards in Malaysia and came back with Radiohead's award,' he says. 'They weren't there, so I put it in my back pocket and sent a photo. I don't think they were best pleased.'

The band were often compared to U2 but Danny had yet to make friends with Bono himself, even though they shared the same vocal coach, Donegal-based Tine Verbeke. Thanks to her, one thing they have in common is a habit of snorting white powder before going on stage. But it's all above board – it's salt, as Danny explained to the *Daily Mirror*.

'Snorting salts – it's actually a singing technique,' he said, adding that he either snorts it or sometimes gargles it to clear his throat and airways before every show. 'It cleans out cavities, it's a natural antiseptic for your throat. Whenever the high notes aren't feeling that high or in the morning you're groggy, you snort salt water up your nose.

We warm up with a nasal shower. We snort salt water up our nostrils and it cuts colds by 50 per cent.'

Pharrell Williams was so impressed by Danny's vocals when they gigged together he asked him his secret to hitting the high notes. But salt wouldn't be enough to prevent Danny from having problems, nor would being a smoker help matters. Just as it looked like their debut album was heading for No 1, he developed a throat problem so severe that doctors told him not to talk. 'I had to text my mates,' says Danny. 'It was a nightmare.'

At the end of the album's first week of release, Danny found himself surprisingly nervous as the band awaited news of the album charts at the west London flat they shared. As he later told *The Sunday Times*, hitting No 1 was the moment they knew they had truly arrived. 'I literally fell to my knees,' he said. 'That was the first time in my life, in my late twenties, that I felt like I had achieved something.

'After any amount of heartache, with people saying, "Would you not get a proper job?" it was the first time I had got a pat on the back. It felt like validation, that what I was doing was right. So my relief that day was unbelievable, especially for something we put our heart and soul into: we wrote it, we recorded it, we produced it, we lived or died by our own sword.'

Things were coming together at the right time but there was that worry over Danny's voice. He had to cope with his sore throat at the worst possible time as the band had festival and tour commitments to honour. He soldiered on, though, ignoring doctor's orders and dosing himself up on medicines to play their V festival gig despite swollen vocal cords.

Mark, whose wife Reena was on the brink of giving birth to their first child Avery, told the *Irish Mirror* that the band were still coming to terms with their meteoric rise. 'It just hasn't stopped,' he said. 'It has been completely crazy. We are humbled because you never expect this.

'Over the weekend we played the V festival in England and we were joking it was our anniversary. Last year we did it with all our gear crammed into a little car and this year we arrived on a huge big tour bus. We went into the tent – it was called the JJB Arena – and it was massive. Our first thought was, "Oh no. What are we doing in here? It's massive." We were worried no one was going to come in but 12,000 people came to see us. You can see on YouTube and you can tell by the look on our faces we were just floored. I couldn't believe it.'

Just a week after the band had held the Irish launch party for their album – again in a church, St Catherine's Church in Dublin – came a gig Danny certainly wasn't going to miss. It was in Marlay Park in Dublin – where he had spent much of his youth – on 19 August, supporting Lenny Kravitz and on the bill beside OneRepublic.

'Marlay Park was really sentimental,' Mark said, 'especially for Danny as it was where he learned to ride a bike and had his first kiss. The atmosphere was electric – it meant so much to us because we have been trying for so long to crack Ireland. It's our home country so it is really important.'

The band were still trying to get their heads round being No 1 in both the UK and Irish album charts. 'It's absolutely crazy – who would have thought that three scumbags from Dublin would get to No 1?' joked Mark.

Now their label wanted to see that success replicated around the world. Plans were already well underway to make them a global priority, with SonyBMG international marketing manager Paul Kindred declaring, 'We see them as the next Maroon 5.' The company flew them to Japan for a whistle-stop promo tour before bringing them back to Europe for an arena tour at the end of September as special guests of OneRepublic.

Their album was launched in continental Europe in early September and Australia in late September, and more UK gigs followed before the band turned its attention to America. The plan was to release it there on 17 March – St Patrick's Day – the following year. 'It just made sense to pick that day, given their background,' says Kindred.

The Script included a cover of David Bowie's 'Heroes' in their live set and were stunned when their version was chosen as the official track of the 2012 London Olympics, particularly as they had originally recorded it as a bit of fun. 'We were just messing around when we decided to record it and it doesn't even really have a proper drum beat,' Glen told the *Daily Record*. 'We really just put it together using a foot pedal for the beat.'

'We wanted to cover it because we just thought it was a great song,' added Danny. 'It's the only cover we've ever done and we can't believe it's just been taken on for the Olympics.'

Mark also revealed that he had asked Danny to be involved in the life of his son Avery, his first-born child. 'I've roped Danny into being godfather,' he told the *Daily Record*. 'I'm expecting him to stand in where I can't. It'll be a real responsibility considering he is still a child himself. The only other responsibility he has at the moment is his utility bills.'

And Danny did take the responsibility seriously. 'I do help him out by taking the baby when he cries and those kind of things,' he said. 'I don't know if Mark knew what he was doing making me godfather as I can barely take care of myself!'

Like the band, Ireland's most revered music expert and RTE radio DJ Dave Fanning admitted he was shocked at how fast The Script had gained popularity. He told Dublin's *Evening Herald* that September, 'I had heard The Script's music at a stage when not many people were even aware of them. Then I went away on holidays for six weeks and when I came back their album was number one in the Irish and the UK charts. I couldn't believe it – obviously they've been years in the making, but the speed at which they've become so successful is remarkable.'

The constant references to them sounding like U2 led, perhaps inevitably, to a story in an Irish paper that Bono was giving Danny 'mentoring sessions' on how to make it big. Danny was quick to tell the *Australian Associated Press* that this was untrue when he was in Oz for a promotional visit at the end of September. 'The story ran back home that apparently I was having dinner with [Bono] last week, which is hilarious because I was in Finland. Yeah, I was having dinner with him last week and he was telling me about all the pitfalls of the music industry, but I wasn't there. I hope the dinner was nice and I didn't get too drunk.'

He then regaled the Aussies with the tale of the first time he *did* meet Bono. 'We met them a number of years ago and Bono and the Edge were great just talking about recording techniques, and just really, really nice guys. I actually ended up making a bit of a fool of myself in front of U2 because I ended up getting really piss-drunk at a dinner we were all at, and I was waving goodbye to the guys as I was walking down the stairs and I took fucking 12 steps on my arse all the way down. I turned around and Bono was actually laughing and pointing at me. So if anyone goes "Do you guys know the guys from The Script?" they'll be like, "Oh those fucking drunks."'

'We Cry' was an early hit with Australian radio stations, so much so that 'The Man Who Can't Be Moved' was added to playlists just a week later. Danny said it was surreal to see fans from the other side of the world singing along to their songs. 'Anyone that's not your friends and family is just a weird experience – people that you don't know singing your lyrics back. There's times throughout the show where it will make the hairs on the back of your neck stand up, literally.'

Danny added that the relentless promotional drive had made him appreciate what it is like for politicians come election time. 'I can only equate it with trying to run for the presidency,' he told the Australian Associated Press agency. 'You're running around kissing babies, shaking hands, meeting people and just trying to spread the message, and the message is music.'

At the very end of October it was announced that The Script had landed their biggest Irish gig to date – supporting Take That on 13 June the following year. 'We only found out a week ago that Take That were doing Croke Park,' Danny told the *Irish Mirror*. 'And it's Ireland's biggest venue – we thought it was amazing that they were doing it so we asked if we could support them. But we were told Take That had already asked for us to be their support act, which is unbelievable and a huge honour.

'At this stage, this early on in our career to get to play for 83,000 Irish people in Dublin, our hometown, is going to be such an amazing night. This has been such a dream of mine since I was a kid and to get to play in front of so many people here means so much to us all.

'We've always been scared of stepping it up a notch – stepping it up from The Sugar Club where we started off, to Whelan's then to The Button Factory and now the Olympia in December. But now we've done the likes of

Glastonbury and the MTV Asia Music Awards which went out to 50 billion people.

'So now this gig with Take That will be the perfect opportunity for The Script to really step up their game and let everybody in Ireland know that we can also do the bigger stadiums. I think it will be a fantastic night. We're all old-school Dublin so nobody is going to get carried away. We're really close friends as well and I think that helps.'

In November the lads came back from Japan after a 10-day promotional tour and, no surprise, they returned victorious from yet another territory. Mark told the *Irish News of the World* that being mobbed by fans had made them feel like The Beatles. 'Hundreds of girls were following us around,' he said. 'Everywhere we looked the same group seemed to appear in front of us, which is a bit scary. It gave us a taste of how The Beatles must have felt when the girls chased them around. We are a very approachable band and love meeting our fans, so it hasn't really bothered us too much. Sometimes fans get hold of our hotel room phone numbers and call us all night, which is a bit mad.

'Just 12 months ago we were recording our album in a shed and now we are getting awards and have thousands of fans following us, it's crazy.'

Being 'big in Japan' is a running gag in the music industry, but cracking this highly lucrative market is actually very hard to do. The Japanese market is the second largest after America, estimated close to $4 billion for 2008 and one of the few mature markets still growing at that time, considering the global economic crisis was starting to hit.

'The top five in Japan for an international act is a major achievement,' Julian Wall, the British Phonographic Industry's director of independent music services, told *The Sunday Times*. 'It's a difficult market to crack because 80 per cent of it is local Japanese repertoire which is pretty high. There's only 20 per cent of it open to international acts and everybody is fighting for a piece of it.'

So when 'The Man Who Can't Be Moved' reached No 4 in the Billboard Hot 100 and was the seventh most played track on Japanese radio between 15 September and 12 October, it was quite a feat to achieve. 'The trio's name is fairly well-known in Japan – a rare thing for an Irish group,' says Kazunari Honke of Hanshin Contents Link Corp, which compiles the Hot 100.

What had helped the band to stand out from the rest? Hirokazu Suzuki, a music critic, wrote in Japan's *CD Journal*, 'Each band member is original, distinguishing them from ordinary new bands. The Script's album is full of rich hybrid sound combining rock's edge and dynamism, black people's beat and groovy quality, pop's pleasantness to the ear, and lyricism peculiar to Ireland.'

On their way back from Japan they stopped off in Monaco for the World Music Awards to pick up the award for Best Selling Irish Act of 2008. And they got an early Christmas present after being told they were going to be awarded a European Union European Border Breaker Award at a ceremony on 15 January, which would be presented by British musician turned TV personality Jools Holland. Other artists being honoured at the awards included London-based artist Adele, with her album *19*, so they were in exalted company.

Danny had been due to visit Crumlin Children's Hospital in Dublin along with other celebrities that Christmas but he had to pull out due to work commitments. Never one to let anyone down, he turned up on his own in the New Year, arriving unannounced with guitar in hand to surprise the sick kids in Ireland's largest paediatric hospital. He made some young dreams come true as he serenaded staff and patients with the band's hits and a sneak preview of tracks from The Script's second album, which he was working on and about to record in the US.

Danny also discovered Bono was supportive of their work when he ended up partying with U2 and Coldplay over the holidays. 'I went to see Coldplay when they played in Dublin before Christmas,' he told the *Daily Star*. 'I was trying to walk to my seat and kept getting mobbed by autograph hunters, so a security guard took me aside and asked if I'd prefer to join Bono in his private box.

'U2 and Coldplay threw a Christmas party after and invited me. I always hoped Bono would be as nice as I thought he was, and he said some great stuff. Out of respect to him I want to keep exactly what he said private but he gave us praise and said he liked the band, in front of Coldplay.'

Danny went along to the gig with a copy of The Script's album, which by that stage had gone double platinum after selling 600,000 copies. 'I thought if there was a chance to mention getting a support slot with Coldplay I should get in there,' he said. 'I was about to hand the CD to [Coldplay bassist] Guy Berryman but he said he didn't need one as he'd already heard it and liked us.'

Having the backing of two of the biggest groups in the world would do no harm to their preparations to try and crack America the following year. More help came at the turn of the year when the *New York Post* tipped the band as ones to watch for 2009 with their 'appealing blend of Celtic pop and R&B'.

They also filmed a scene for hit MTV reality show *The Hills* which showed them being showcased to record execs by star Audrina Patridge. A spokeswoman for the band said they were thrilled and added, 'This is a huge deal. *The Hills* is a massive show and it is watched by a large number of people.' Indeed: with an American audience of around 4.3 million viewers per episode, *The Hills* was MTV's most successful show and aired all over the world. 'All my friends are fans,' says Danny, 'and my sisters when they heard, they went bananas.'

At the end of January, *Business Wire* in the States reported on the 'highly anticipated' debut album of The

Script due for release on 17 March and gave details of the important appearances being lined up for the promotional campaign. 'The album's arrival is amplified by news that VH1 has just handpicked The Script for their powerful *You Oughta Know* artist campaign scheduled to begin in March. Recent *You Oughta Know* artists have included Adele, Leona Lewis and Duffy, all of whom are 2009 Grammy Nominees.

'Kicking things off for The Script in America are huge national promotional campaigns with both CBS and VH1. Tracks from the album are being featured in the hit CBS show, *The Ghost Whisperer* as well as in VH1's new show, *Sober House* – which will feature The Script's music all season long.

'On Saturday, 31 January, The Script will perform tracks from their forthcoming debut on The CBS *Saturday Early Show*. Look for the band to perform a special St Patrick's Day show on release day in NYC at The Highline Ballroom.'

America was waking up to The Script, and for Danny it was justification for all the hard work and personal pain that they had poured into their record. 'In retrospect, I don't think the first album would have been as poignant a statement if we hadn't been going through that torture at the time,' he told *The Sunday Times* in September 2010. 'For us, to be able to accurately describe emotions, that was the point of The Script, and you can't write about these things if you haven't experienced them.

'And as far as our lives go, the pinnacle was that album, the opportunity to put this on paper and to have the world listen to this.'

CHAPTER 7

MIXING IT WITH
THE BIG BOYS

In March 2009 it was announced that The Script would be returning to the festival scene in their homeland, with an appearance at Oxegen that July as part of a stellar line-up that included Kings of Leon, Blur, Lady Gaga and The Killers. 'I'm very, very nervous,' Danny told the *Irish Independent*. 'I'm apprehensive, but I have to say it's going to be a fantastic night. If last year is anything to go by, we're going to have one hell of a night. We're third from the top so it's a nice, nice slot. It's going to be dark, we're going to have a light show. It's going to be a special night.'

Danny, who said he was dying to see Blur in action, also recalled that the previous year they had played on the new band stage, not expecting anybody to show up. 'The Kooks were on playing on the other stage and we were kind of thinking we're an Irish act – are they going to show up? Will they even care? And we walked out to a sea of people! They had tricolours flowing in the air and that really made us literally step our game up. To be playing on the main stage this year … I'm just imagining last year multiplied by 100. It's going to be crazy.'

'It was like a scene from Italia 90,' Danny recalled to the *Irish Sun*, 'and we were revved up to go on and give the best show that we could. Now we are performing third from the top on Friday night, which is incredible. Going on before Blur and Snow Patrol is something we are really having to pinch ourselves about.'

Ahead of their album going on sale in the US, The Script released 'The Man Who Can't Be Moved' as their debut single there. *VNU Entertainment Newswire* championed it: 'The Script arrives in the States with a sure-fire success story as the best-selling new band of 2008 in the United Kingdom and Ireland, a number one album and a World Music Award. But more so, launch single "The Man Who Can't Be Moved", which is already a smash in a dozen nations, possesses an easy, breezy vibe, a driving melody packed with one monster hook after another.

'Lead singer Danny O'Donoghue is awfully dapper, destined to charm the pants off of top 40's female demo[graphic]. The Script's self-titled album is due 17 March – from the same label that ably broke Adele.

'Programmers, if you're not moved by The Script, kindly turn in your FCC license. You're simply not serving the public interest.'

Despite their soaraway success, Danny admitted that he was still finding it surreal to adjust to the A-list showbiz lifestyle. 'I went to Elton John's birthday party and ended up standing by the bar with Mark Wahlberg and Seth Green standing behind me,' he said. 'Snoop Dogg was there too and I was dying to meet him, but I couldn't get past his bouncer. I swear to God I was a nobody at this party.'

On St Patrick's Day – a big deal in many American cities – the lads found themselves on NBC News' *Today's Toyota Concert Series* for an interview and performance of 'The Man Who Can't Be Moved' to promote the album. The anchor Natalie Morales told them that '*The New York Post* are today calling you a pot of gold' and said they reminded her, like so many would tell them, of U2.

Danny said the comparisons were a 'huge honour', adding, 'You know, we started this thing in a very small shed in Dublin right next door to where Guinness is brewed on James's Street. So here we are in New York today, on what a great day as well, you know?'

Success on the awards front continued that same night when they were honoured back home at the Meteor Music awards, winning Best Irish Band and Best Irish Album for selling more than 600,000 copies at a time when album sales were being decimated by illegal downloading. The band joined the party by video link. 'We are absolutely gobsmacked and thrilled,' Danny grinned. 'We would have loved to have been there on the night. This is just the most amazing feeling.'

People were queuing up eager to work with them. James Morrison was the latest in the long line, calling them 'the best act to come out of Ireland in years'. 'I'm a big fan and so to do a song with them would be amazing,' he told the *Irish News of the World*. 'They are really nice lads and their music is great. They have really set the charts on fire with their superb tunes.'

Another famous fan was American singer-songwriter Anastacia, although she was enticed by Danny's looks as much as his music. 'First of all he's hot, second, he sings like a dreamboat – and that Irish accent is irresistible,' she purred. Pixie Lott too admitted she was keen to meet him that summer when they shared the bill at the Isle of Wight festival, describing him as 'quite nice-looking'. It seemed like every woman he meets falls for Danny's charms – another swooning over him that summer was Taylor Swift. 'I have a crush on the singer from The Script,' she admitted. 'He is cute.'

Mixing in the top showbiz circles now, the boys attended Adele's 21st birthday that May, armed with booze from Bono as well as a gift of their own – a cigarette lighter. 'Bono couldn't make it, so he sent us a huge bottle of champagne and some Guinness,' Danny told the *Daily Mirror*. 'We wanted to share it with Adele to celebrate, but she has gone off the booze – we were gutted. So we bought her a silver lighter with a shamrock on one side.'

At the end of May details of their first headlining national tour of the States were announced, on the back of playing sold-out venues supporting Grammy Award-winning pal Adele. The 14-date tour would kick off in Seattle on 30 July and end in Washington DC on 17 August, taking in major cities like New York, Chicago, Boston, LA and Philadelphia along the way. Meanwhile 'The Man Who Can't Be Moved', which had reached number one in five countries, was holding strong in the Top 20 on Adult Radio and their appearance on MTV's *The Hills* propelled their album up the iTunes chart to No 15.

The Script were already stoked at getting to support Take That at Ireland's biggest venue, the gaelic football stadium Croke Park in Dublin that June. But they were even more astounded when U2 asked them to support them at the same venue the following month. 'I think there will have to be a truckload of Pampers brought in for that gig,' said Mark when it was announced. 'We are absolutely shitting ourselves. This is going to be the big one.

'We grew up looking in amazement at venues like Croke Park and listening to the songs of U2,' he told the *Irish Sun*. 'Now to have Bono and U2 saying that they're fans of ours is completely surreal. The idea of playing Croke Park is sending chills up our spines. They have sent us a couple of letters and notes saying that they are fans. It's a huge boost to us as a band – we'll have to hold on to them all!'

Danny was given the opportunity to write an article for *The Guardian* in June in appreciation of U2. In fact, it was more an out-pouring of admiration for Bono – it was clear that Danny viewed his elder statesman in high regard: the young frontman was in awe of his world-famous countryman.

'I saw Coldplay at Christmas, and they were magical. But I'm frightened for Coldplay, because for years they've been seen as taking the crown from U2, and to see this huge industry beast that is U2 just now arising from its slumber.

'Now I'm seeing from the industry side what a band like that awakens in people. Everybody ups their game because U2's back on the scene: the shit bands are shaking in their boots, and the good bands are like, "Bring it on!" Everybody from merchandising people to songwriters to A&R men, they love U2: it's like U2 are most people's reason why they got into the industry.

'You can't plan a career like U2's: it's luck mixed with emotion mixed with honesty mixed with everything – the stars just aligned for a band to be that successful. They walk through the industry with their heads held high, they treat everybody with absolute respect, from the tallest in the record company to the smallest. And that's what makes U2 a great band.

'There are a lot of lead singers who would almost take the Bono formula, and who'd say, "What you have to do is, you've got to go over to Africa, and you have to care about this and care about that, and then if I'm seen holding a baby from an orphanage I'll achieve that same stature and fame."

'They're trying to think about it – Bono just does it. The other lads in the band dislike the fact he's so open about it, but I think people buy into that honesty – that he's ready to hold a peace sign up while he's standing there with George Bush, that he's willing to wedge himself into these situations for the publicity of people who have no voice.

'And it's such a commendable thing, especially in today's day and age, when everybody's so fickle. A lot of new artists don't realise the great ones do it through honesty, through following their hearts, not following trends.'

In June 2009, Danny told the Australian paper *Herald-Sun* that the ultimately bitter experience of Mytown had them prepared for their second stint at fame. 'Having been through the mill once before we were definitely a hell of a lot more prepared, we sharpened our tools up for this time around,' he said.

By this stage their album had amassed 1.5 million sales worldwide, and their hard work jetting around the globe playing and promoting themselves was reaping its rewards. 'We know all our hard work is paying off if you just knuckle down,' Danny told the paper. 'A lot of bands lose sight of that. They think, "Why am I here in a conference room playing to five people wearing suits?" They're the tastemakers, the people who decide what song is going to be played 15 times a day for three months. It's a necessary part of what we do.'

And the remarkable thing is that despite their success,

they were often considered a faceless band early on – people recognised their music and enjoyed it, but knew little of them initially.

'People call us "the band nobody knows" and that's great,' said Danny. 'We made a conscious decision not to have ourselves on the cover of our album. We wanted the music to speak for itself. We've achieved this success with nobody knowing who the fuck we are and what type of a band we are. We've sold 1.4 million records now and we have a huge amount to go.

'We only just got our very first magazine cover, *Hot Press* in Ireland. We're only really coming on the radar as a band now. The anonymity that comes with it tastes very good. Your songs are doing damage around the world and you can still walk down the street.'

Danny thought that their heartfelt emotional lyrics had established a connection with their fans, but insisted that he has no interest in politics. 'I say leave the politics to politicians and the religious stuff to priests. "Breakeven" is a love song and you're saying pretty much the same thing as any love song has already said, but finding a little spin on that is the art for me.

'There are certain issues that unify thousands of people. You have to find those feelings and sing those truths. This guy walked up to me and said, "You just said in three and a half minutes what I've been trying to say to my wife for my entire life." Those are the moments that make all the hard work worthwhile.

'The band's diverse musical scope is no accident. We

represent the iPod generation – people who aren't loyal to a genre. My iPod has everything from Bob Dylan to Boyz II Men, Babyface to David Gray. I think our album is like one big iPod.'

Fresh from touring with Adele, and with supporting Take That and U2 next up, The Script were in demand to join some of the biggest artists in the world. 'It's hard to think of any band out there today who can support U2, Adele and Take That and have the crowd accept them,' says Danny. 'Not blowing our own trumpet, but it's a great place to be musically. We're not stuck in a genre, nobody's pigeonholing us.'

Not only did Danny get to support Take That, the die-hard Manchester United fan got to meet one of his heroes, a certain Republic of Ireland legend, after their gig at the Old Trafford cricket ground in Manchester. 'Roy Keane was there and I was told he wanted to meet us after we performed,' says Danny. 'We were playing for 45 minutes basically for Roy Keane in Old Trafford. It was like the shoe was on the other foot – I'd watched him my entire life and now he was coming to watch me!'

As they got ready to play Oxegen, on home soil in July, which Danny said would 'probably be bigger than Croker', they were already planning the second album to keep the momentum going. 'We're not in the slightest bit worried ... all that hunger and humility poured into the first album, it didn't go anywhere,' he said. 'We can't wait to put the tap into that keg and bleed ourselves dry.'

After the Oxegen show, where the crowd welcomed

them back as conquering heroes, the band landed a slot with Beatles legend Paul McCartney. As opening act, they would make history as the first music act to perform at Citi Field Stadium, the new $650 million home of the New York Mets baseball team, on 17 July 2009.

Danny couldn't believe he would be rubbing shoulders with another idol of his. 'Macca is one of the greatest songwriters ever,' he said. 'Oddly enough we got a call from our management saying, "Paul McCartney has requested to play New York with you. What do you reckon?"' says Danny. 'And we were like, "What do we reckon? We're in!"'

Danny told the *Irish Mirror* that they felt like Forrest Gump when they met the former Beatle. 'We were having a discussion in the dressing room about what to call Paul McCartney. We didn't know whether to call him "Sir Paul", "Paul" or just "Macca" but the next thing the door flew open and he walked into the room and greeted us all. He just randomly walked in and we nearly fell over and fucking died. He was an absolute gentleman and he was asking us all about our lives. We were surprised he knew so much about us. I thought that was great.'

Macca also had words of wisdom to share with the band as he sat and chatted with them for half an hour. 'He goes, "What is it like for you guys, coming from being a very small band? As the Beatles had to go through that,"' said Mark. 'The way he said that alone, we were like, "The Beatles!"'

'When you meet anyone like [McCartney], you don't

say anything, you just let him do the talking,' Danny told the *Edinburgh Evening News*. 'If anything, he'll teach you a thing or two. He was just teaching us about being on stage and how to make 80,000 people feel like they're on stage with you. What a man – we're massive Beatles fans.'

Danny was honest enough to admit that he thought – just as with their experience of Christina Aguilera in Mytown – that McCartney wouldn't know who they were, never mind stop by to see them in person.

'In the industry people have support acts they don't even know,' he told the *Northern Echo*. 'I was fully prepared for that but Paul knew everything about us and he had a copy of his album and had sent ten people to check out our act. He said, "I picked you guys out because I've been hearing so much about you. I've got a new album coming out, have you heard anything about it?" Come on! How down to earth is that? And then we opened at the Shea Stadium [now Citi Field] with him in the US. Just us and him. I knew I'd be happy if I died the next day.

'That's always on the resume now. He drank shots with us backstage and watched our set from the side. It was mad – he knew all the songs.'

'Our last two years are full of Match of the Day highlights,' Danny added to the *Courier-Mail* in 2010. 'Here am I having a conversation about meeting and supporting Paul McCartney. He was so personable and approachable, no security guards. He said, "I know you've come from a very small stage and you're on a big stage in a short amount of time – how does that feel?"

'We were trying to tell him how much we appreciate it without sounding like a total knob-end. So we asked him about how he did it and he said, "When we did it, it was weird because we were separate from each other on stage for the first time." You think, "This 'we' he's talking about are the fucking Beatles!" We sat there in awe as he was willing to tell us about how the Beatles used to record, how to tell stories to the crowd.

'Here's this little Irish chancer who's tried to get his foot in the door all me life and I'm on stage saying, "Ladies and gentleman up next, U2" and "Up next, Paul McCartney." Seriously, it's fucking crazy.'

The pressure got to Danny on one of the nights – he was left red-faced after an embarrassing mix-up with his keyboard buttons as he introduced each band member to play a solo. 'When it came to my turn, I was supposed to play a piano riff on the keyboard but I hit the wrong button and it came out as drums,' he winces. 'It sounded rubbish. In front of 50,000 people and a Beatle! That was bad.'

Back again on NBC News' *Today's Toyota Concert Series* to perform 'Breakeven' a few days after their gig with Macca, the band were left blushing as co-host Tori Spelling dubbed them 'AKA the cute boys'. Kathie Lee Gifford asked how things had changed since they had last been on the show, just four months earlier.

'It's been incredible, you know,' said Danny. 'We've

been on a European tour, we supported Adele. We got the opportunity then, two nights ago to open up for Sir Paul McCartney in Citi Field. We have to say, this show has definitely catapulted us off on to better things as well, so thank you very much for having us on again.'

For Danny, getting to perform before his idols U2 and McCartney was 'surreal'. 'Those moments in your life are ones you'll remember for the rest of your lives and you'll tell your grandkids,' he says.

In between the big arena support slots, The Script came back to Dublin for a five-night run of more intimate gigs at the Olympia Theatre. 'It was an absolutely incredible gig,' said Danny after the first night. 'We've brought this act all around the world and we've hopefully fine-tuned it just in time to give Ireland the best shot we could give. This has been a milestone for us. We've lived in the shadows of U2 our whole time in Ireland.'

When it came to the big one – opening for U2 at Croke Park – it was everything Danny hoped it would be and more. 'U2 are our heroes,' he says. 'Supporting them in front of 82,000 people had a kind of gladiator effect. As a musician, you feel alive.'

Danny admitted to the *Courier-Mail* that they were nervous about the reception they would get as they played on the imposing stage, which had a giant rig called 'The Claw' casting an imposing shadow over it. 'It wasn't a claw that night, it was a sweaty palm,' joked Danny. 'We were fucking shitting it! It was amazing; 80,000 people, our own backyard.

'We started "The Man Who Can't Be Moved" and the whole crowd took over the song and every hair on the back of my neck stood up. In my mind I'm thinking, "U2 are watching this."

'We thought we did a great gig, then 20 minutes later U2 come on and wipe the floor with us. Watching them is like a religious experience.'

Despite the newfound wealth and trappings of fame, Danny confessed that he still bought his underwear in Irish budget store Penneys, or Primark as it is called in the UK. 'I was in a shopping centre in Artane [in Dublin] recently, buying my socks and jocks in Penneys, when the girl behind the till recognised me and I ended up signing autographs and taking pictures with her and her friends,' he told the *Irish Sun*. 'The shop assistant looked at my credit card and shouted, "It's Danny O'Donoghue from The Script!" All the shoppers came over looking at me buying my jocks – "Eh, size small, ha ha!"'

He might buy his boxers in Penney's, but Danny admitted that the band weren't raking it in, despite their fantastic record sales, as much as you might think. 'There's not a load of money floating in,' he told the same newspaper. 'It'll be a while before royalties and that come in, but as the band is getting bigger, the overheads are getting bigger. We literally pour everything we earn into a joint account, which goes back into our shows and music. The only way of giving people a good show is pumping all our money back into the business.'

Danny told Australian newspaper *The Courier-Mail* in

September that rather than young female fans throwing themselves at them, it's often older women who have been the worst wannabe groupies.

'It's usually their mothers would you believe,' he revealed, before sharing the gory details of one indecent proposal. 'It was a meet-and-greet and these two mothers had their children with them, and as they were being ushered out, in front of everyone including kids, they yell out: "You can tag-team both of us ... me and my friend!" I mean, can you believe that?'

In February 2010 at Ireland's Meteor Music Awards there was a shock as U2 failed to win anything, but The Script were back among the honours for the second year on the trot and this time they were there to revel in the limelight. The band won the Best Live Performance category and Danny told the audience, 'This was the one we wanted – there are no words. We supported U2 in Croke Park, we didn't think we had a chance at all – it's fantastic.'

The boys often make themselves a four-piece on tour, recruiting session bass player Ben Sargeant for gigs, as when they returned – on St Patrick's Day again – for a stint on NBC News' *Today's Toyota Concert Series*, this time hosted by Alan Thicke, dad of Robin Thicke, and they were congratulated on the success of 'Breakeven'.

'It's going crazy,' Danny said. 'You know, since we were last on, it was a year ago. You guys were literally one of the first ones to ever ask us, invite us on a show. And since then, God, it's just skyrocketed. I mean, it's been an amazing year. We've supported Paul McCartney, supported U2. And now the song "Breakeven" is rocketing up the American charts. You can't dream dreams like this, you really can't.'

Alan was pleasantly surprised to learn that Danny had 'wrote a song with Robin some years ago' and asked them about their belief that 'soul comes from anywhere'. Danny replied: 'It's not a black thing, it's not a white thing, you know? We believe that soul is a human condition, you know?'

The show hosts then gave the guys a welcome surprise for a happy St Patrick's Day: 'You guys hit gold. So this is a certificate to show your "Breakeven" hit … Certified gold, you guys. Congratulations and happy St Patrick's Day.'

'Breakeven' was a breakthrough song for The Script. Even back in January 2010 John Mayer had predicted its success, tweeting, 'Every band with a single this year has a mission: beat "Breakeven" by The Script. Oh, yah … good luck.' It would put them on the map across the pond, but it was a slow burner – they had already begun making their second album by the time the song eventually hit No 1 in the US.

'We'd finished working the album in the UK and Australia, there'd been five singles,' Danny told the *Courier-Mail*. 'Then we got word "Breakeven" had got some traction on the American charts. We've beaten Snow Patrol's "Chasing Cars" for the slowest burn to get from the bottom to the top – 36 weeks. This song three little young fellas from Dublin wrote in their darkest moment is in the American Top 20. Last time around we were knocking on people's doors, now people are knocking on ours.'

That record-breaking nine-month climb to hit the summit of Billboard's Adult Top 40 chart saw them sell 1.8 million downloads and propelled their debut album to 313,000 sales by May, according to Nielsen SoundScan. That success came even though, remarkably, the song was banned by some radio stations in North America, as it was deemed to have controversial, even blasphemous lyrics.

'I guess it is [controversial],' Danny told Canada FM. 'I don't know why. Because the lyric was "I just pray to a god that I don't believe in," it got banned from a lot of Christian stations in the US and Canada. But I don't think we're that controversial. You know, we're not talking about science and faith or politics and religion.'

As Danny had told the *Irish News of the World* in January, the band saw themselves more as storytellers than musicians. 'Our music has become about much more than tunes,' he said. 'Our forte is storytelling. We've been getting pats on the back from people for singing about normal things like heartbreak, tragedy and triumph. You have these words that you wrote at your darkest time, in your darkest hour, late at night in Dublin – and people relate.'

Despite their relentless work schedule, The Script were still writing songs for others, with *American Idol* winner

Kris Allen recording one of their songs, 'Live Like We're Dying'. 'It was great,' Danny told the *Courier-Mail* in 2010. 'Many radio stations had to decide if they were going to add "Breakeven" or "Live Like We're Dying" to their playlist that week. But both were our songs so we won. That song is up to two million in the US, so we've sold four million songs there.'

They were back again on NBC in May 2010, this time with host Matt Lauer, when there was a sea of green to honour them as they took to their summer concert stage for the very first time. 'You made your American television debut on this show back in March of 2009,' said Lauer. 'And 14 months later, you guys have exploded.'

Danny replied, 'We haven't really had time to take stock of what's happened in the past year, you know? From three guys from a really small shed in Dublin, as we said on the very first day we got here, to these dizzying heights that we are now.'

'Anything you miss about the anonymity that you used to enjoy?' Lauer asked. 'Because that's gone, those days are over.'

'No, I don't miss any of it,' replied Danny honestly.

The *New York Post* reported that Danny had met Hollywood actress Cameron Diaz at *Today*, with their source telling them: 'Diaz was working her charms on Irish band The Script, also on *Today*, where she ran up and told them that she was a big fan. She wanted to know when they would next be on tour.' Their spy reported that Danny and Diaz swapped telephone numbers ... but Danny wasn't interested – he was already in love.

CHAPTER 8

LOVE IS IN
THE SCRIPT

Little did Danny think, as he began thumbing through piles of photographs of gorgeous women to find one to star in his new music video, that he would come face to face with an ex-girlfriend – and his future love – in the same sitting.

After shooting the videos for their first two singles in New York and Los Angeles, the band wanted to return home to their Dublin roots for the third, 'Breakeven', because people new to the band's work were starting to ask if they were American. They needed a leading lady to star as a love interest opposite Danny and had been sent a selection of pictures of stunning women from local model agency 1st Options. Danny was gobsmacked when there before him was a picture of a beautiful brunette he used to go out with. 'It brought back a lot of feelings and emotions,' he says. 'I said all week, "I hope it's not someone from Dublin we know."'

Danny pours his life experiences and emotions into his songwriting, so there was good reason for him to move on from the portfolio belonging to his ex – their break-up was part of the inspiration behind the song. 'It was surreal because the song is partly about her,' he told the *Daily Telegraph* in Australia, 'so I was, "Nope, next, no way!" She's an actress and model back home and obviously her agency put her up for it. It's one for the books, I'll say. It could have made for some real on-screen tension.'

When Danny finally picked out the lucky lady to star in the video – a young woman by the name of Irma Malinauskaite, but who goes by the shortened, catchier Irma Mali – he was blissfully unaware that it would be the start of a beautiful romance. That said, it was clear he was smitten from day one: 'The lead girl, Irma Mali, is amazing and tall like me,' he enthused. Irma was a model in her native Lithuania before moving to Dublin at the age of 20.

Danny admits he can't help himself when it comes to flirting with beautiful women, and it would be no different on set with Irma. 'If you're single then flirting is a great thing because it just means that you're available and you're out there looking,' he argues.

Just one week after filming the video – which was shot around Dublin, including the docks and rock pub Whelan's – Danny admitted to the *Irish Mirror* that he was secretly dating a mystery Dublin woman. 'I've started dating someone but I am taking things really slowly,' he told the paper. 'We are going to just have fun and see what happens as right now it's really hard to say, "OK, I'll be here on a certain day", or to say that I will be around at any stage.

'To really get into a relationship you have to give it time – and time where you are actually in the same place. So we are just playing it by ear – when I get time off we get to see each other. We are trying to keep things nice and light for now as you really need to give a relationship what it deserves and proper time.'

Danny refused to tell the newspaper Irma's name and maintained that the relationship was not yet serious. 'I can't tell you that – I'm not saying anything,' he said. 'But when you meet someone that you don't mind waiting around for it's fine. I do find it very hard, as there is only so much that you can talk to someone on the phone. You have to be around that person for a relationship to flourish and so things aren't serious at the minute but yes, there is a mystery Dublin woman.'

Danny was smitten by Irma's beauty the minute he clapped eyes on her but he didn't know that Irma's ex-boyfriend Marius Simanaitis, the father of her then six-year-old daughter Nikoleta, was believed to have had links to organised crime gangs in his native Lithuania.

Barely six months after Irma began dating Danny, martial arts and cage fighting obsessed Marius was shot in the head in a Dublin apartment. He was found dead in a pool of blood with a gun in his hand. Irma was distraught at the shocking turn of events.

Marius' family still maintain he was murdered, but at the inquest into his death on 12 January 2010 the coroner ruled that he had killed himself. The *Irish Independent* reported that 'a request for an adjournment of the inquest was denied by the Dublin County Coroner after police raised fears that witnesses' lives were at risk. They revealed their Lithuanian counterparts had uncovered a number of threats to the witnesses involved in the case. It is understood that the dead man may have had links to organised criminals in his native country of Lithuania. The jury returned a verdict of suicide from a single gunshot wound to the head after witnesses told how Mr Simanaitis had shot himself at his apartment off the Navan Road, north Dublin, in March last year.'

The inquest heard that both Irma and Marius' brother Donatas had raised serious doubts that he had shot himself, saying that he was too devoted to his daughter Nikoleta. 'There is more to my brother's death than meets the eye and I will not rest until I find out what happened and who was involved,' Donotas said.

Donotas's solicitor Rody Kelly Corrigan said his client had been 'deeply affected' by his brother's death and requested the adjournment of the inquest so that he might attend. But Superintendent John Quirke told the coroner, Dr Kieran Geraghty, it was his belief that an adjournment would put the lives of the witnesses at risk. 'If I adjourn the inquest, it might increase the risk,' Dr Geraghty said.

'This is an inquiry, not a criminal trial. I can't put the lives of these witnesses at risk.'

Gardai (Irish police) had carried out an extensive investigation into the death of Mr Simanaitis and concluded that it was not suspicious. Witnesses at the inquest told how Mr Simanaitis had been talking about his daughter 'with his head in his hands' on the night he died.

Witness Lukas Tiskevicius told how he was in the room, drifting off to sleep, when Simanaitis had shot himself in the head. They had been having drinks at Simanaitis' home earlier in the evening and he was staying the night there along with friends, Jurgita Balsiukeviciute and Vilius Muznikas. Balsiukeviciute said that she had become distressed earlier in the night when Simanaitis had produced the gun, which had a silencer attached to it, as well as a crossbow, and begun playing with them.

She said she had been upstairs asleep with her boyfriend, Muznikas, when Simanaitis shot himself but she had not heard it. She was awoken by Tiskevicius, who she described as being in a 'state of panic and shock'. Tiskevicius had told her that Simanaitis had shot himself.

A week later Donatas was given High Court permission to challenge the inquest verdict that Simanaitis had committed suicide. Donatas claimed that he and his family, who believe he was murdered, should have been able to attend the inquest where the suicide verdict was returned.

It was a stressful time for Irma but with the love and

support of Danny she was able to cope and her newfound showbiz lifestyle with Danny was a pleasant distraction. In fact, it was rubbing off on her. In February she told how she had enrolled at The Gaiety School of Acting, inspired by her part opposite her new lover in The Script's video for 'Breakeven'.

'I'd done commercials before but doing that video made me realise how much I wanted to act,' she told the *Irish Independent.* 'It made me think theatre, TV and films. I suppose I will have to see what happens. I had always wanted to act but my modelling work got in the way. In the last few months I decided if I was going to do this, I needed to do it now. I went to see the people in The Gaiety School and joined up. I'm really enjoying it.'

She would later win small roles in short productions and indie films, including *The Callback Queen.* 'My day is so short between modelling, acting classes and my daughter, but I love it. It's better than sitting at home doing nothing.'

Well, she wasn't always sitting at home doing nothing. By March Danny was telling the *Irish Sun* that he was 'besotted' by his lover. 'She's a real girl-next-door type and I'm besotted by her,' he admitted. 'I can't stop looking at the video just to watch her – she's amazing.' He also said he was only sorry he didn't ask Irma out on the day of filming. 'The more I watch the video the more I wish I'd made my move that day.'

The boundaries were established early on, with Danny glad that his girlfriend had some understanding of the lifestyle he leads. Even though hundreds of adoring women throw themselves at him on a regular basis, 'Irma is not the jealous type. She knows that signing autographs is part and parcel of what I do.'

But as Danny knows, and no doubt secretly enjoys, being the good-looking singer in a rock band does mean that women will swoon over you. And it wasn't just fans, but also many a celebrity encountered along the way, among them Hollywood actress Cameron Diaz.

'My girlfriend Irma went nuts when she read about Cameron,' Danny said in July 2010. 'She was lovely and told us she was a big fan, but that was it. Irma knows how much I love her.' Danny said, 'I get to say "no" to some of the most beautiful girls in the world, who would not have come anywhere near me if I was not in the band … They would not have looked twice at me in the past – maybe even slapped me across the face if I'd approached them in a club.

'There are no hotter women than the ones in Australia. I got whiplash when walking around and turning my head all the time. I've been going with a girl for two years now and my… are we in trouble?'

Things were getting serious. By the time of the new school term in September they were, dare it be said, almost something of a family unit. 'We've just taken my girlfriend's daughter to school,' he said. 'That was fine, but there was crying over the weekend when they sent me out to get some of the clothes! A pair of shoes that maybe didn't fit so well.'

Danny and Irma even had their own coping mechanism when it came to acclimatising back to normality after months away on tour – booze and hotels.

'As a musician, you feel alive on stage,' he told the *Daily Record*. 'That's what you live for. You fear it but still have to walk out into it. It's a big adrenaline rush and when you go on tour with the band and do a headline gig you get that all the time. When the tour stops, you just go home and are chilling and kind of going, "OK, when are we going on stage, what am I doing?" And it's very difficult.

'At first you have to allow yourself time to kind of reabsorb yourself into normal life and it takes a while because you're just living for the next tour. I try to wind down with wine sometimes. My girlfriend definitely thinks I go a bit crazy for the first few days after a tour and, for me, I think I'm best maybe to stay in a hotel for one or two days just to get back to normal.'

At the end of October, Donatas – the brother of Irma's former boyfriend, Marius Simanaitis – obtained a High Court order quashing the inquest verdict that Marius had died by suicide. Mr Justice Peter Charleton ordered a new inquest be held.

The *Irish Independent* reported that Irma was adamant after the death of her partner that he could not have committed suicide. 'He was utterly devoted to his daughter,' she said. 'He adored her and was not the sort of person to forgo his responsibilities. I don't want to believe he was murdered because of any implications that this realisation brings, but one thing I do know is that everything I know about Marius from our time together says he was definitely not the sort of person to kill himself.

'For a start, he was always very happy and positive, and had such an open, optimistic and ambitious outlook. In all my time with him, he never showed any signs of depression. I have known Marius since I was 14 and he has never taken drugs, never been convicted of any crime and never associated with criminals. I cannot believe he was found with a gun because I never saw any guns when I was with him.'

By the summer of 2011 Danny and Irma were still in love and revealed the secret to keeping their long-distance relationship strong – Skype. They would use the internet webcam programme for 'Skype dates' and spend hours declaring their love in online chats.

'You should see some of our Skype dates,' he told the *Irish News of the World*. 'You do what you can to make it work. Anyone who's in the industry, where they're away from their loved ones a lot, knows you have to keep it interesting and be contactable. I talk to my missus two or three times a day about the same mundane things as everybody else.

'She's an amazing person who, no matter what, is there for me. I'm blessed to have her in my life. If I had a weekend off she would take me skydiving. She is mad and wild, my missus. It is going brilliant but we are taking things easy.'

Early on, Danny tried to lay down a marker by telling reporters how he was very much in love with Irma and that she was 'over the moon' about his new TV job. 'She thinks people won't know what to expect from me,' he said. 'She knows what a big thing this is.'

'She's really good at not making things difficult,' he added to the *Sun's Fabulous* magazine, 'because working in this industry can be really difficult. I'd be more worried about her getting chatted up. Every relationship has to start with trust. When I was younger and didn't know what love was, things were different. Now I'm absolutely a one-woman man.'

Naturally there were also questions as to whether this new TV star had any plans to tie the knot with his 'incredible' girlfriend of four years.

'Both our careers are enjoying a really fruitful period right now,' he told *Look* magazine. 'It's hard being away from her, but we know there's a day when this is all going to work out. I send her flowers, and every other night I meet her for drinks in the Skype Bar. It's literally like online dating!

'It's going perfectly. It's going in a great direction. We're both busy and we've both got our own lives. That is why I fell in love with her. She's such a confident person.'

The opening of the second inquest into the death of Marius Simanaitis coincided with Danny's time on TV, although the inquest had been adjourned at Dublin Coroner's Court and was expected to take several months. His brother Donatas said, 'Marius did not really talk about why they split up,' he said. 'He just said that their paths went in different ways. But their break-up was amicable. They shared looking after Nikoleta. Irma met Danny after she had split up with Marius. Danny has come to Lithuania with Irma to bring Nikoleta to visit her grandmother.

'He seems a good guy. He met Marius's family and was polite to my mother. Nikoleta speaks Lithuanian but obviously Danny does not, so we do not talk to him about Marius's death.'

CHAPTER 9

SCIENCE
& FAITH

In the music business there is always talk of the 'difficult' second album, but The Script were in a better position than most. They had been working up to this point for years. Lessons had been learned. They knew what it took to make a hit record and while they were enjoying their success, they had been conscientiously plotting their second album to ensure follow-up success.

Mature enough to have a business plan for their career, they had been writing material in the meantime so that they could hit the ground running to kick on from what had been a brilliant 24 months. Inside two years, The Script's debut had sold more than two million copies and gone eight times platinum in Ireland and three times in the UK. A total of 2.2 million singles had been sold in the US, with stints on top shows, not least *The Hills*.

Many awards had been received at home and abroad, from the Meteors to bringing the house down at the World Music Awards in Monte Carlo. U2, Take That and Paul McCartney had taken them on board for massive stadium gigs, and they had played Glastonbury, Oxegen and T in the Park in their own right.

But Danny, Mark and Glen are not men to sit still. By 2010 they were ready to strike while the iron was hot and build on their explosive entrance to the music scene. *Science & Faith* would be the title of their second album. 'We're trying to be a mirror to our own generation, and that seems to be a topic that comes up now and again – science and faith, two massive subjects that can't live without each other,' said Danny.

It wasn't the only thing they had been working on. In a repeat of the situation surrounding their debut album, Mark was due to become a father around the time their second album would be released in September. Two years previously he had been forced to rush from the Dublin launch party to hospital for the birth of his son. Now he was gearing up for a 'gentleman's family' with a girl on the way. 'It's becoming our lucky omen,' he joked. 'So maybe expect a baby every album release date.'

But there was a serious side to the new material. The band always pour their heart and soul into their work, and this album would be etched with the emotional heartache of losing their loved ones, Danny's dad Shay and Mark's mum.

'A lot of our songs are like therapy sessions,' explains

Danny. 'We go in and say you'll never believe what happened last night and it finds its way into the music.'

It wasn't just the songs that would be poignant. Danny had plans to have a permanent gesture on the cover to pay tribute to their late parents. 'We are thinking of putting a woman and man's hand together on the front of the album sleeve,' he said. 'I'd love to remember my dad who passed away before we had success and Mark's mum too. So we were thinking of putting both of their faces inside the hands.'

Danny was clear that that the 'difficult' second album cliché didn't ring true for them. 'People have been saying it for ages now,' he told the *Nottingham Evening Post*. 'It's just one of those words, I guess, that people say and I don't really understand it. For us, we found the first one really difficult. We'd been trying for a long time to get it right and finding our own sound, something that we were comfortable with. It's about hitting that point where we all look at each other and go, "I don't think we can write any better right now" and I think that's exactly the way we feel.'

With the first album the band had been forced to return home from the US because of those family tragedies. This time around, they came home to Dublin after two years away to work on their material from the off – but instead of returning to Ireland as conquering heroes to celebrate their success and begin work on their second album, they found a recession-decimated country on its knees, with people out of work, losing jobs, houses and even their marriages.

'It was one of those things that just hit us in the heart emotionally,' Danny told the *Daily Mirror*. 'It almost pales in comparison when you are telling your mates what you have been up to and they are saying, "That's great, well done, but I've just spent my last money coming out here and I have no job."'

'I was shocked to the core,' he added to the Australian *Daily Telegraph*. 'These people got me to where I am. My sister gave me money when I didn't have any, mates drove me to rehearsal with my keyboard jammed into the back of the car, and here I was in a pub celebrating what we had achieved. It just paled in comparison with what people were going through.'

Danny was in a pub with friends when he was approached by a fan, an older man, who told him he hardly had two pennies to rub together after losing his job – and he had spent the last money he had in his pay cheque to go and see The Script play live.

'I didn't know him,' Danny told the *Sun*, 'but he said I'd given him the best send-off ever. I was confused. He explained he had been made redundant three weeks before but that night had come to see us. He said we played every note like we meant it, like he hoped we would. Then he bought me a pint. He had no job or money but insisted on buying me a pint to say thanks. I don't care what critics or anyone says. A stranger telling me that is the best reaction you can hope for. And that's all that matters to us.'

When Danny recounted the heart-tugging tale to his

band-mates, they got together to write 'For the First Time'. 'Every time I sing it, I get the same feeling in my stomach,' says Danny.

'We went back home to Dublin and all we could feel was this sense of loss,' Danny told the *Sun*.
'We wanted to celebrate our success and being home but there was fear in the air. The recession had hit everyone hard. People were getting their cars and possessions repossessed. But then, after the panic, there came a positivity from this hardship. People realised that just because you're losing your car doesn't mean your family has to split up. It was time to reassess what was important. A lot has been lost but the best thing is that people have found each other emotionally. It makes you stronger. That's why our new album cover shows two people holding hands.'

Although the song was inspired by hardship, Danny told the *Irish Mirror* that its message was also one of hope. 'Now that we are stripped of the momentary things, I think we are actually having a great moment – we are going back to the table and getting together,' he explained. 'We have the lyrics in this song, "Drinking cheap bottles of wine and shit talking up all night." I really feel we are going back to what is important and that's why we wrote this song.

'There's a lot of hope in this song because there is a magic moment where the girl is standing in the dole queue. It's such a bleak picture and yet she has a massive smile on her face and that's because she feels she has someone she has connected with again. That's what this song is about.'

'If you look at Irish history and everything we have been through it's in the psyche,' Danny added to the *Sunday Mail*. 'As kids we grew up around funerals where there would be a big party at the pub afterwards. We grew up around balladeers, people singing songs about their troubles and when Ireland was in trouble, it was always put into song and that's a big reason for the storytelling nature of our songs.'

Thoughtful themes like this were proof positive that the band had taken a more measured and mature approach to their second offering. 'We weren't trying to come with the album a certain way,' he told the *Daily Record*. 'We had a mark not to fall below and the "difficult" second album is only difficult if you think of it differently in your own head.

'The first album lets you do what you want and for the second one, you listen to opinions. And the more you listen, the less it becomes about musicality. We didn't listen to outside influences but played a waiting game and waited for our emotions before we wrote. It really is a continuation of our first album with a little bit more age and wisdom under our belts.'

To star in their video for 'For the First Time' the band recruited Bono's daughter Eve. Not that she needed a leg up – she had already landed a role alongside Sean Penn in the movie *This Must Be the Place* and would go to win more Hollywood roles. The video shows a tearful Eve writing a letter to her mum and dad in Dublin, saying she's missing home. 'We're not a band that does something in small measures,' said Danny. 'She was available and we thought we'd get some serious attention if we did this.'

It was another sign of the developing relationship between Danny and his musical hero, but the most striking move was made by Bono. When Danny and co were headlining the Roseland Ballroom in New York, Bono sent them some champagne and Guinness with instructions on how to make a Black Velvet and a note saying, 'This town isn't big enough for the both of us – so I'm leaving.'

Danny believes that in order for the searing honesty of his lyrics to ring true with fans, the band have to sacrifice any notion of acting or looking cool. 'To be honest we don't really care what anybody thinks of us,' he says. 'We left cool behind a long fucking time ago. We did! To give honest and heartfelt music, you have to.'

'Especially in this day and age!' he told *The Times*. 'The industry is like, "Let's blow this face up as big as it possibly can get." Then, bang! – it blows up! But that's what we're so proud of. We don't like the way we look. We're not an image-driven band, we never have been. We're not a self-gratifying band either. We don't put our own image on our own albums just so people know it.'

For *Science & Faith* The Script would again have an album launch with an exclusive showcase gig for selected media. This time it was fittingly at the Guinness brewery in Dublin, with Mark's house and their Madhouse studio where they learnt their trade in its shadows. 'We'll play them some of the old stuff, some of the new stuff, and get them all so pissed they'll hopefully like what they hear!' joked Danny ahead of the big night.

Yet, as Danny would tell the *Sun*, ultimately they do not care what the critics think of them. As long as their fans continue to love them, that's all that matters. 'We've never bothered about the critics,' he said. 'Our music is emotional and honest. It's who we are and we can't fake it. We're never going to please everyone. If you try to, you have a hard life. I just try to please our fans. We try to please ourselves first and satisfy our own wants and needs and everything falls into place.

'Who wants to be credible and only play to 30 people in a pub? Some people call it selling out but I call it smart because we've never compromised our sound. We still create our own sonic thumbprint.'

Danny told the paper that it was the time spent with Paul McCartney that had helped prepare them for the next stage in their career. 'He told us about when The Beatles started to play bigger stages and how they learned to reel crowds in. A masterclass in performance,' he explained. 'Then he told us about telling stories to keep the crowds captivated. We watched him that night on stage. He told the crowd how he had written the song "Here Today" about what he would say to John Lennon if he met him now. Everyone was spellbound. I'll never forget that and that's why we are always as honest with

112

our songs as we can be – even if they don't portray us in the best light.'

Danny was firmly of the belief that with two albums of anthemic arena-rock songs, allied to the experience of playing with Macca and U2, they were now ready to spread their wings and go it alone as headliners.

'We loved touring America and supporting U2 and McCartney was amazing, but now we want to play those stadiums as headliners,' he declared. 'We're not shy about saying we want to be huge, but that doesn't mean we want to be famous. We love our music and want it out there. We're not scared of hard work. We spent 10 long years practising, being the tea boy in studios. That was the most important period for us and we will never forget that.'

Danny has always been remarkably candid and honest regarding how the band developed their sound – and how they see nothing wrong being mainstream. For him there is no shame in being successful: they spent many years mastering the business side of things as much as the musical side, so he feels they have earned the right to reap the benefits.

'If you're in any way smart as a band or as an entrepreneur in the industry, you have to realise that you need to make your music palatable in order to get it out,' he told *The Sunday Times*. 'Not to earn money but so that you can get your art to the biggest number of people possible. I guess we started out trying to emulate all the other records we heard on the radio, and it ended up not sounding like anything else. We tried to copy our heroes and got it a little bit wrong, but in essence got it totally right.

'People talk about a meteoric rise to fame, and it has been a crazy couple of years, but we've been unsuccessful much longer than we've been successful. If we go back to that tomorrow, it's no skin off my nose.'

Their slick production, poignant lyrics and boyband history have all at times caused The Script to be viewed as more pop than rock, but any flak they get from critics, the Twittersphere or anywhere else also fail to graze Danny's snout.

'To be emotional and heartfelt, to sing about some of the things The Script sing about, like tragedy and triumph, and dealing with that, you can't be cool,' he said. 'You're opening your heart, you're opening yourself up for criticism. Anybody who comes out and wants cred and kudos, fair play to them, but we don't give a shit.'

'We are a mass-market band,' Danny added to the *Irish Times*. '*NME* reviewed our album and gave us 3/10 – no surprise there; we're hardly a shoe-gazing band, are we? We exist in that grey area of pop, that sort of rock/pop divide, and we know we are marketed as a pop act. Our heroes are U2 and Coldplay. We like A-ha. We can't spell it out much more for people.'

Finding fame later in life has had many advantages for Danny and the boys. Having that vital experience of the harsh realities of the music business has meant that they would be aware when it came to the financial side as well.

Of all the rules in The Script, having a frugal approach to their earnings was etched in stone at the top of their commandments.

'Rule one of being in a band – know where the money trail goes. I've heard too many horror stories down through the years not to want to know everything that's being done in our name,' he told *Hot Press* magazine. 'People assume because we're number whatever in the American chart that we're millionaires – far from it!

'I never realised until reading the *Bono on Bono* book how close U2 were to bankruptcy during the eighties and into the nineties. It was because of that desire to do things bigger and better than anyone else.'

While Danny really only cares what the fans think, he is also open and honest when it comes to critiquing himself: 'I've written some amount of crap over the last 10 years,' he said in September 2010.

He even told Australian paper *The Age* that their second album wasn't better than their first, but instead was on a par. 'I don't think it's better than the first album, but it's as good. We have hit a plateau ... where we have exhausted every avenue of being as emotional as we can,' he said. 'I'm very nervous. I've had such an amazing whirlwind the past two years and I'd hate for it to stop and to think that I wrote a bad album and that's why.'

But one thing he is passionate about is their unique sound – born in Ireland but schooled in America – and a rare example of an Irish rock/pop group engaging with a heady and eclectic mix of contemporary soul, hip hop and R&B sound as well as rock.

'The reason Ireland is proud of us is that we don't have violins in the music,' he told *The Age*. 'They love that we're not standing in a big field of shamrocks in all of our videos. We take our influences from soul music, from rock and pop – we don't put a fiddle in our music. That's why Irish people are so proud we compete with Maroon 5 and The Killers on our terms. We're not a novelty act. We are not trying to be something that we're not, we're just trying to be ourselves.'

They were, by this stage, soaring to heights they could have only have dreamed of at the beginning, Danny told the *Irish Times* in September 2010.

'We started The Script from a shed in James's Street, and there have been times over the last two years when I've been literally stopped in my tracks by what has happened to us. When we played the Sugar Club way back, I used to hide behind the microphone stand I was so scared – and you're thinking of this when David Letterman is introducing you on his show. You're going to yourself, "Jaysus, we're just three lads from Dublin, we shouldn't really be here."

'Having had the lean times, I'm not going to start complaining that I haven't had a day off in eight months. I woke up the other month and it was my birthday and I was in New Zealand and I was just thinking, "This is mad."

'And then weird stuff happens – you hear that 28 radio

stations in the US have banned your single "Breakeven" because it contains the line "I just prayed to a God I don't believe in", and you wonder if you should worry about that or just leave it.

'The only thing that has annoyed me is a certain Irish daily paper that swept through where we are from in Dublin – stopping old friends, knocking on neighbours' doors, even talking to the window-cleaning man – trying to get stories about us. They even somehow blagged their way into a neighbour's house, leant over the wall and took a picture of "the shed where it all started for The Script".'

Danny is simply someone who loves, lives and breathes music, and of all tastes. His favourite songs on his iPod include 'Hometown Glory' by Adele, 'Babylon' by David Gray, 'Substitute' by The Who and 'The Times They Are A-Changin'' by Bob Dylan. He says if he could form his own 'fantasy band' it would be made up of Sting, The Edge, Paul McCartney, Keith Moon and Elton John.

When it came to The Script's music, however, it was back to Dublin to launch *Science & Faith* at St James's Gate, the headquarters of Guinness behind the streets where Mark grew up and the band learnt their craft. They flew over the great and the good from the media and to add gloss to the proceedings, their new single 'For the First Time' went to No 1.

A week later, in the first week of its release, their album followed suit in Ireland, shifting nearly 14,000 copies inside seven days, leaving Danny 'completely floored'.

The feat was repeated in the UK with entry at No 1, ahead of new albums by Linkin Park, Robert Plant and Phil Collins.

'We believe soul is not just a genre of music – it's a human condition,' said Danny. 'We have put ours into this music and are humbled by the response the album has received.'

Danny reckoned that the gruelling two-year experience of promoting their first album to get the band established across the world would serve them well this time around. 'Irish people are always ready for a challenge,' he told the *Courier-Mail*. 'This time around we're a little more prepared for it.

'First time we got our heads blown off by the amount of promotion you do and the amount of countries you see. This time around I've actually started boxing because I've started going to the gym. Physically, I need to be in a good shape to deal mentally with the onslaught of the next two years.'

Danny also told the newspaper that rather than becoming divas or saying 'no' to more demands from the music business, his approach was: bring it on.

'Actually, I'll say no to a lot less things,' he explained. 'You realise how precious you are with your music first time around doesn't really matter. You want the most people to hear your music as possible. You might not want to go on certain shows or be in certain magazines because it's deemed uncool. This time around, fuck cool. We love the fact our music is heartfelt and emotional. If

Left: Danny on the keyboards at Oxegen July 2009.

© *Damien Eagers*

Right: The Script opened for U2 on their 360 tour concert in Croke Park, Dublin, on 27 July 2009, the last of three nights for U2 at the venue.

© *Vipireland.com*

Above: Danny back with the crowd at Oxegen in 2011.

Below: Leading the crowd at the same festival.

Inset: Nerves, what nerves? Backstage at Oxegen before meeting the crowd.

Danny O'Donoghue (left) with Mytown boy band colleagues Terry Daly,
Mark Sheehan (now in The Script) and Paul Walker at a publicity shoot in
London in 1999.

© *Getty Images*

Above: The Script, from left to right: Glen Power, Mark Sheehan and Danny in Dublin, December 2008.
© *Gareth Chaney/Collins Agency*

Below: The band, with Laura Whitmore from MTV, for the Oxegen 2009 Festival.
© *Arthur Carron/Collins Agency*

Danny pictured with girlfriend Irma Mali in Galway, August 2011.

Above: The Voice judges line up in March 2013: Reggie Yates, Danny, Sir Tom Jones, Jessie J, will i am and Holly Willoughby.

© *Rex Features*

Below: The Script perform at the third and final day of the Radio 1 Big Weekend in Derry, Northern Ireland in May 2013.

Credit: David Fitzgerald, photograph courtesy of Independent News & Media.

you want to be heartfelt and emotional, you can't be cool at the same time.'

Ever-optimistic Danny even has a philosophical and pragmatic approach to the bane of the industry – illegal downloads. His view is that rather than damage the band, they helped them on their way to selling two million copies.

'We've heard the statistics that it's five to one, for every person who buys it five people download it illegally. You can't combat that. I think they're quite important people, the illegal downloaders. They're like the tastemakers. They want everything first but they'll also tell five people, and those people go out and buy it – we're more reliant on them. And we've sold out shows. Music is so readily available online, but you can't download the live experience, living and breathing these songs live.'

Danny told the *Sun* in September 2010 that the one thing about The Script is that they have kept their feet firmly on the ground as they travelled the road to stardom. 'Nowadays a lot of bands are image-based – being in a scene, dressing a certain way,' he explained. 'Their music seems to be second to their perfume lines and what they are. That's not what music is about.

'If you're in a band with Irish people, the moment you get a big head they will get their pins out and go, pop, pop, pop. You won't find a picture of ourselves on the front of a CD – would you do that if you looked like us? We're not doing this for fame and self-gratification.

'We aren't about to let anything go to our heads. We

want to enjoy and appreciate everything that happens. It has been a long road but it's worth it now. We want to leave a legacy of songs, number ones, but also earn good money that will take care of our families.'

The band were set to tour on the back of the new album, which by the third week of September was number one in Australia as well as in the UK and Ireland. The dates included two homecoming gigs at Dublin's O2 the following March. The band broke box office records by selling 60,000 tickets in just 40 minutes, forcing promoters to add extra dates in Dublin, Killarney and Belfast.

The arena tour would also see the boys take in dates across the UK, and Danny admits that despite their experience and stature, nerves still kick in before they take to the stage. 'It doesn't matter if it's something in front of ten people or thousands – it can just hit you,' he says. 'I'm always fretting about forgetting the words or tripping up or something.'

That aside, he couldn't hide his delight at The Script being headliners in their own right, to quote their hit single, for the first time in cities such as Aberdeen, Glasgow, Nottingham and London. 'Our first arena tour is now upon us and we can't believe this magic run we are on,' he said. 'First and foremost, we are a live group and this stage is something any band can only dream about. We are so humbled that people are putting us in this position and are eternally grateful.'

A tired Danny told the *Nottingham Evening Post* that

life couldn't get much better for them at this stage. 'I guess the only complaint you can have is that you have no time off, but that's the least of your worries when you're on to a good thing,' he reasoned. 'We really can't believe ourselves; that's why we've been out celebrating, hitting it hard. We're chomping at the bit to get back out there and play tracks from the second album. Nottingham's going to catch us when we've done 15 shows so you will be getting a slick performance when we're all in our stride.'

That October Danny spent his third consecutive birthday in Australia, flying in on the day of his 30th ahead of the launch of *Science & Faith* at Luna Park's Big Top in Sydney. 'It's like home there anyway and my brother Darren lives in Melbourne with his family,' says Danny, before a follow-up tear-up at the Oxford Art Factory, where they caught up with an old pal.

Boyzone star Ronan Keating has made a name for himself on Aussie TV screens as a judge on their version of *The X Factor* and had made plans to join the lads for some post-show beers. Not only that, he arrived with some of his contestants from the show and, more importantly, 40 burgers from Hungry Jack's, which were devoured by the band – they never eat before a gig, so they were starving by the time Ronan landed in.

But while Mark and Glen joined Ronan and co for a huge drinking session, poor old Danny had to miss out on the fun after damaging his voice by pushing himself too far with his performance. 'I lost my voice so I had a cortisone shot in my arse and a B shot and went back to the hotel and had a cup of tea,' said Danny.

Glen told the Aussie media that being in a rock band with a pin-up lead singer has its benefits: 'I get to hit on the girls that Danny knocks back.'

Ever the showman, Danny loves being the centre of attention so it's maybe no surprise that he says he fancies a crack at acting, after being bitten by the bug when starring in The Script's music videos. 'I love acting,' he says. 'If a part comes up for at all, skinny Irish guy who writes love songs, I'm sure I'll get it. I just need Angelina Jolie as my leading lady.'

The band next announced dates for their first US headlining tour – 20 gigs in big cities like New York, LA, Chicago and Boston – which would kick off a year later, in October 2011.

Science & Faith would not be released in the States until January, but before then they would continue to promote and build up excitement ahead of it going on sale across the pond. In November Danny said the most important gig for them would be at the Aviva Stadium in Dublin, home to the Irish national rugby and soccer teams. 'There are going to be 60,000 people there, our own stadium, playing our own music – we are calling it the homecoming,' he said.

The band made a conscious decision to price their stadium show tickets lower than any other act because Ireland was being strangled by the recession. 'The good thing about these shows is we are undercutting every other act,' he said. 'Tickets are starting at about €40, us being The Script – a working man's band, so we want to keep the prices low.'

Mark told the *Irish News of the World* that they could easily identify with cash-strapped victims of the economic downturn as they'd been there themselves. 'We know as much about recession and hard times as the rest of the country,' he said. 'Believe me, we signed on the dole for longer than we've been successful. Any musician knows exactly what it's like to sleep on a mate's couch, scabbing money and getting lifts to rehearsals.'

Danny added that, because they know what it is like to scrape a living, they are being sensible with their cash as well as pumping it back into their stage productions to enable them to grow as a band – but also thinking of their fans. 'The bigger we get, the bigger our gigs get,' he said. 'And we have to pay for them. We pay ourselves a modest wage and then put everything we make back into the band.'

So it is little wonder then that The Script get such unequivocal support in return. They beat U2's blockbuster *360* tour to win the Best Live category at Ireland's Meteor awards that year; they drew a bigger crowd to the 2009 Oxegen festival than co-headliners Oasis; and their second album had already enjoyed five weeks at No 1 in the Irish charts.

'The nation is behind us,' Danny told the *Daily Telegraph* that November. 'I've seen things at Script gigs I never thought I'd see, grown men climbing on each other's shoulders, singing along, tears in their eyes ...'

As if to underline their good guy credentials, they combined their love and compassion for their fans with a cut-price gig that would also raise cash for charity. The special 17 December midnight gig at Dublin's Olympia Theatre would cost just €10 with the proceeds going to Temple Street Hospital and the Simon Community.

'This gig will give us the chance to give something back to our fans who have supported us at the beginning and give them a chance to help us do some good in the community,' Danny told the *Irish Mirror*. 'Ireland has been such a champion of our music from the start, we wanted to close the year there and give something back. We are honoured to be able to help in this way and look forward to it. It will be an amazing night in our home town.'

Danny likes a beer. He smokes. And he certainly loves women. All fine rock star qualities, but he is different – he's serious about his craft, and his music comes first. 'We're really not that interesting,' he says. It's all about the music for us. It really is. If you want to know about our personal lives, listen to our songs. We write about our lives.'

It's ironic now, given that he would go on to become a coach in the TV show *The Voice* and One Direction would become one of the biggest bands on the planet, but Danny told the *Daily Star* he was no fan of *The X Factor*. 'How many years has it been on now and how many successful artists [has it produced]? The diamonds are few and far between,' he argued. 'It's easy to go from singing karaoke to being on the stage and being famous. The hard work is what's important.'

After enjoying Christmas and the New Year it was full steam ahead to push *Science & Faith* as it was released in the US on 18 January 2011. The band landed appearances on such top-rated TV shows as *The Late Show With David Letterman*, *The Ellen DeGeneres Show* and *Jimmy Kimmel Live!* and it paid off – the album went straight to No 3 in the Billboard charts after shifting 49,310 copies in its first week.

The Script were working hard – and playing hard. A gig in Orlando, Florida was followed by the band and their crew drinking the venue dry, working their way through minibars at their hotel, ordering carry-outs from the nearest outlet and jumping fully clothed into a swimming pool. It's not always the image they portrayed back home.

'We decided not to do the celebrity circuit,' says Danny. 'The result is that, back in Britain, we're seen as sensible, maybe a bit boring. As long as we're selling albums and selling out shows, that's OK with us.'

Mark told *The Sunday Times* they were happy to hold on to that image, in an interview over the phone from the States. 'We're ordinary blokes who don't want to hang out with a load of dickheads who think they're better than everyone else,' he said. 'So we go to pubs with real people who don't have cameras and aren't trying to sell stories. We don't pretend to be anything we're not.

'I've watched bands say they're downing vodka on stage when it's just water. We'd rather be honest. We're happy to admit that we make pop music because we know we do it really well. In the UK, that means we're deemed to be lightweights. Over here, it's different. Nobody cares if we're cool. People come to see The Script for a big night out, to sing along and cheer themselves up.'

The pub plays a special role in Irish life and being Irish helped The Script stateside in their early days as they played the Irish pubs in all the major cities. 'We assumed only big cities like New York and Boston had Irish bars, but they're everywhere,' Danny told the newspaper. 'It was fantastic for us. People who hadn't heard of The Script, who were just out drinking, saw us live and started telling their mates. That's how we caught on. On the Irish scene, word spreads like wildfire. Even in places like Florida, where they don't really give a damn about the Irish, we were packing out cocktail bars.'

This was at the same time they were playing to thousands in the UK and Ireland, but they were wise to the fact that in the States, you need to build from the bottom up.

'We were living a double life,' said Glen. 'In Ireland and the UK, we felt like proper pop stars. Then we'd come here and be back to playing pubs. Straight after we did a five-night stand at the Shepherd's Bush Empire, we flew to Miami and played to 400 people in a pub where we set up our own gear. The same week we supported U2 at Croke

Park, we played a tiny Irish bar in Wisconsin because the local radio station was hammering "Breakeven".'

'Our egos were all over the place,' added Mark. 'We're not the type to get big-headed, but playing pubs definitely brought us back down to earth. Then we got the call from McCartney.'

'Having met McCartney, we'll never get big-headed,' said Danny. 'He taught us how to behave. He walked into our dressing room with no entourage and spent 20 minutes talking to us, explaining stuff he didn't have to and giving us advice. In this business, you have zero longevity if you treat people like arseholes.'

Danny was not impressed by Jarvis Cocker, the lead singer of Pulp, and took a swipe at him in February after both acts signed up to play that year's T in the Park festival. 'I am not a big Pulp fan,' Danny told the *Daily Record*, as he accused the band of reforming solely to cash in on nostalgia. 'Jarvis Cocky. I'm not into him at all. I don't like his style. I don't like his music. I won't be steering clear of him, but he should be steering clear of me.

'I have watched his career. I'd like to think Pulp are coming out with a new album or that he wants to really do a job in the music industry, but I am sure they will release a single, do a tour, make their money and go home.'

Danny also blasted Cocker over his famous stunt at the Brit awards in 1996, when he stormed the stage and shook his bottom at Michael Jackson as he performed

'Earth Song'. 'The audacity of Jarvis Cocker to think he is important enough for people to give a damn what he thinks,' he added.

The Script would play their UK and Ireland headlining shows before hitting the festival circuit, also including Oxegen and V Festival, ahead of their US tour. The band also took their music to some far-flung corners of the world, with a gig in Manila in April and Johannesburg and Cape Town in June.

The band went down a storm on their European tour and often allowed themselves to dabble in the rock 'n' roll lifestyle with a good boozing session as a reward after a storming set. 'The shows have all sold out and the second album is seeping into people's consciousness,' a worse for wear Danny told the *Irish Mirror* the morning after a gig in Switzerland in March. 'They come out and sing all the brand new songs. It's great,' he said of the reaction to *Science & Faith*.

'We're talking about religion and politics of the heart,' he explained. 'The give and take, the yin and yang of modern relationships. It's the science of men who think they know best, and women being very faith-based and leaving it all up to mother nature, I guess.

'I think our success has been down to hard work. I don't think we're any more or less talented than any other band. I just believe that we've put the grind in, being in different parts of the industry since we were kids. We're not reality TV stars or *X Factor* kids. We knew that a band in their late twenties trying to hit the scene would have to do it the old-fashioned way, playing gig after gig after gig.

'The song is king. After that, it's hard work that determines how much you are going to get out of it. Anybody who wants to be a lead singer always has the ego that thinks the room is never big enough. I get quite emotional on stage. To be able to give the best representation of your songs you have to get quite emotionally on edge, I think. It always ends up being engaging and entertaining. There's not too much smoke and mirrors.

'With us it's four lads wanting to play good songs for you. We always wanted to play bigger places, but didn't realise that we would be doing that in such a short period of time. To have U2 and Paul McCartney turn round and ask us to support them in the same year was a dream come true. But I know that I could be back on the dole in 10 years' time. You can't take it for granted.'

The band played in their home city's O2 Arena in front of thousands of adoring fans and Danny showed his true colours with a tricolour sewn into his jacket. After their Irish shows, The Script embarked on an eight-month tour covering the UK, Australia, Hong Kong and the US.

Ahead of their first UK gig in Nottingham, Danny declared that they had learned from their stints supporting U2, Take That and Paul McCartney about what makes a headlining show in an arena work. 'From the big productions of Take That to the stripped-back nature of Macca's gigs, you learn from all of them,' he told the *Daily Star.* 'The biggest thing we got from watching their shows is how you draw an audience in so it's like they're on stage with you. It's all about storytelling. That's the art of a good song and show. We saw it night after night with Take That, who acted like normal, real guys, really approachable, and that is how they reeled in the crowd.'

Danny said that the album hitting No 1 in the UK and Ireland was obviously among his career highlights thus far. But it was cracking America that really excited him. 'When *Science & Faith* got to number three on the Billboard charts, that was a big one,' he said. 'A lot of people measure success by how well you do in America. We've been to the US 23 times in two years.'

Their reputation continued to grow across the world. They were selling more and more records and playing bigger venues all the time, but still kept their feet on the ground. 'Irish people have inherently got one foot on the ground,' says Danny. 'You may try to get the other one up but there'll be people to pull it back down. Also, it's happened to us later in life. We're not 16, we can hopefully control it.'

There were no lavish cars or houses bought either. Danny treated himself to a professional Canon camera costing £3,000 – his biggest splurge – but put it to good use snapping everything from TV appearances to the support band on tour. But he knows that years of hard work building a successful career could vanish in an instant. He even dreams about it.

'I was sitting in a pub waiting to make a great suggestion about how we could make the tour better and, just as I was about to speak, the chair disappeared and I fell on my arse,' he says of a recurring dream. 'I don't know what it means. Dreams often mean the opposite of what they seem like, don't they? It's a precursor of something different. It probably means my ideas will save the whole tour.'

Ahead of their gigs the band join together in a chant – 'fail to prepare, prepare to fail' – to pep themselves up. 'It can be scary though, and it's not like we can rely on costume changes and pyrotechnics,' Danny told *The Independent* backstage at their Birmingham show. 'I was reading an article about Elbow today, who have also just started their first arena tour and they were having the exact same issues. If it's taken you a long time to get to the arena, you're going to be worried about how you can connect with people at the back.

'Now when we go on stage, you'll see us taking the moment in. We're genuinely thinking how brilliant it is. I'm going to take those extra couple of seconds on stage and enjoy it because for a while there, we didn't really think we were going to make it.'

When you're filling arenas, who cares about what others say? The Script were having too much fun to worry. 'Personally, I love it,' says Danny. 'When critics say bad things it galvanises our fanbase and they go after them, they really do.'

After sold-out shows in Melbourne, Sydney and

Adelaide in Australia with rapper Tinie Tempah as support, The Script returned to the UK, but they were lucky to escape unhurt after a serious road collision on their way to perform at the Radio One Big Weekend event in Carlisle. 'We had a crash last night, a bad accident,' Danny revealed to the *Daily Record* on 16 May. 'We were driving along, having a drink and, whack, someone hit us. The wine was all smashed over the floor. It's the worst thing that's happened yet on tour and it was pretty serious. It was the first collision we've had on our tour bus.'

Thankfully the band emerged unscathed and just two weeks later they were breaking new ground with their first ever gig in Canada. The Toronto show was a sell-out. Danny told *Canada AM* that they were blown away by the chart success of their second album. 'You can't ever expect it,' he said. 'We've been saying for a long time you can't dream dreams like this. We were writing a few songs in a small, little shed in James's Street in Dublin. And to travel around the world, to be playing these shows – we had a sold-out arena tour back in the UK, and now we're kind of on our North American leg of it – it's unbelievable. You really can't write the script – pardon the pun. But you can't write a script like it, you know.'

As the band moved on to the US, Danny had no problem telling the *Boston Herald* on 7 June that fans are more important to them than the opinion of critics like *The Guardian*, who said they had an 'incredibly pedestrian' sound, or *Rolling Stone*, who described *Science & Faith* as 'soaring, melancholic and treacly'.

'We've been dragged though the press,' said Danny. 'We haven't been given critical acclaim. At every turn, at every corner, there's someone wanting to say, "They're not real, they're fake." You can throw everything you want at us, and we'll still be here. It doesn't matter if we don't get a four-star review. Who cares? There's three million people around the world who bought our albums, sing the lyrics, come to the show, leave comments on our Myspace or Facebook page to say this music has meant something to them.'

Having a thick skin is a tool of the trade for Danny, not least because it took years of hard work and knockbacks to get where they were, and a dedication and commitment to a huge workload.

'It's been an incredible struggle for us and it still is,' said Danny. 'As much success as we've had in the last two or three years, we've had it being away from our family and friends. It's a whirlwind, a whole other type of lifestyle. For people to have the mentality that it's overnight success, I have to say it was the longest, darkest night of my life. It's the analogy of the graceful swan gliding atop the pond. No one gets to see the legs underneath racing away 1,000 miles an hour.

'When you start a band, you're in the mind of a magical "what if?" but when you're living it, it's a whole other thing. You're getting your wildest dreams, but also your wildest nightmares. The yin and yang. People say I don't know about the recession. Fuck you, man! I've been sleeping on people's couches for the past 12 years. I'm more qualified as a musician to talk about the recession than a lot of people. The industry that we're in now, it's attack-minded. Just shut up and enjoy the music. I got into music because I got into a song that turned me on. I think the optimism is what the band is about.'

At the end of June they played Johannesburg (their biggest headliner yet, with a crowd of 18,000) and Cape Town but before that they cruised around the Caribbean on a boat as part of the VH1 Best Cruise Ever trip, which also included Maroon 5, a band they are often likened to.

But spending so much time on the road can get tedious for three guys (four if you include touring bassist Ben Sargent), even if they see themselves like brothers. To lighten the mood, there's plenty of practical jokes and messing about on the Script's tour bus and elsewhere.

'We've shoved Glen into an icebox,' Danny told NBC's *Today*. 'It was like a square foot and he basically fit into the whole thing. I think it's up online. You can go check it out.'

Danny also admitted the song 'Nothing', which they were set to perform live on the show, was actually inspired by his own habit of drunk dialing. 'It's not my problem with alcohol,' he said. 'It's actually my problem after the alcohol. Everybody knows this: you know – you jump on Twitter, your Facebook or, like I do, text a lot.'

'We play a game called Inappropriate Frisbee all the

time,' Mark offered. 'Wherever we are – we could be in the elevator or we could be on the bus – we'll literally be playing Frisbee everywhere we go.'

CHAPTER 10

THE HOMECOMING

Here it was. Of all the gigs on their tour, and there were many, this was the one they were most excited about. Their triumphant homecoming was a 60,000 sell-out at the national stadium, Dublin's Aviva. 'I know I'm in the band, but the sense of "Wow, it's an Irish band filling an Irish stadium with Irish people" is there for me too,' Danny said of his 'pinch-me moment'. The homecoming would mark a big week for the band, as they would follow it up by headlining the 80,000-capacity Oxegen festival.

It was fitting that the band's biggest show so far as headliners – more than three times bigger than Joburg – would be at home. Supporting U2 at Croke Park two years earlier had left them certain that they had it in them to strike out on their own into the arena of, well, arenas. 'You can have goals and dreams as a band,' Danny said.

'We jumped off the stage, looked each other in the eye and said, "This is ours for the taking."'

Despite the enormity of their biggest show to date, Danny was not apprehensive about it. 'For some reason – I don't know if other lead singers suffer from this – but I get less nervous the bigger the gig,' Danny told the *Irish Mirror*. 'I have no idea what that says about me as a person but I am sailing into this one like it's a breeze – it's no problem at all. But be honest – if you were shitting yourself so much that you can't do the gig then I think you are at a bad stage.

'I think we are ready for it. We were apprehensive before going out on stage with U2 and Paul McCartney and even the Croke Park Take That gigs. There was almost a feeling of, right lads, hold on to your hats because it is never going to happen again. We will be chewing off this sitting at a bar when we are 60 years old so take stock of it now.

'We have put in the time, we have supported a lot of massive acts out there and we are feeling comfortable enough to step out from under their wings and see if we can fly ourselves. You grow up compiling lists of things you want to achieve before you are a certain age, and there's a couple of those that I will be getting crossed off in the next week, which is fantastic.'

They'd had two No 1 albums, a world tour and the biggest shows they'd ever done in their home country. But Danny felt they still had a lot of hard work ahead of them, and they wouldn't be resting on their laurels.

'Every band thinks as soon as you get a deal it's easy, but that's when the real work starts,' he told the *Irish Mirror*. 'As hard as I thought my life was before we got a deal – being a broke musician and sleeping on people's couches – the main problem we come up against all the time is that when it's so saturated with pop music, it's very easy for people to put us in the same bracket with every new batch of bands who come out that year.

'And it is hard to try and get out from underneath that. But a lot of people are realising now that we are a hardworking band who have been on the pub circuit, the garage circuit – we have paid our dues. We don't have famous relatives, we haven't come off the back of a reality TV show, we're doing this the old fashioned way – great songs, great gigs.

'Fame hits people in all sorts of different ways. We have always believed that fame is a magnifying glass to the person you have always been. So if you are an asshole, you get to be 10 times the asshole. If you're cool, you get to be 10 times as cool. Being Irish you innately have your head in the clouds but your feet on the ground. That's the great thing – no matter how much your dreams run away with you, your feet stay on the ground and if you get ahead of yourself, someone else will hold them down there for you.

'If you let the fame monster swallow you up you would be sitting in its belly a very unhappy person. But that doesn't happen with us – fame has just accentuated the love we have for our families and friends for keeping behind us for such a very long time.'

One other person keeping Danny's feet on the ground was his girlfriend Irma. 'I have an amazing girlfriend who gives me the strength to go off and do what I need to do,' he said. 'She understands that without music I am nothing and she pushes me in that direction at every given opportunity. And it's great for her as she gets a bit of a break from me too.'

Danny says that the band had grown so close they were like family, sibling rivalry included. 'At the end of the day we are brothers and we kill each other over things. We are all headstrong, savvy people trying to negotiate this industry in the best possible way we can. We all look at it as if we were on *Who Wants to be a Millionaire* – we are basically at the third question right now but we have to confer on every answer. Sometimes people know the answer, sometimes they don't. We do argue but it's because we all want to achieve the same goals.

'If we weren't such a tight unit The Script would have been over a long time ago. When you get to the fame game there are a lot of people pushing and pulling you and they look for the cracks. We have heard of other bands where people are coming and saying, "Oh you could sell a million if you did this on your own," or "You're a much better singer than he is," and it's all bullshit. No one has any magic ticket to making it and because we are so close knit, no one will be able to come between us. We're all too Dublin 8 for anything like that to happen.'

As much as The Script were loved by fans, success had also made them a target for haters – and hackers. As they basked in the glory of their triumphant Aviva show, on 5 July web hackers managed to post hoax claims on the Sony Music Ireland website that Danny and Mark had died after the gig. The unsavoury cyber attack read: 'Backstage Danny O'Donoghue and Mark Sheehan requested rope and beer. They locked themselves in the changing room and refused to leave. The staff eventually broke in to find the two talented musicians hanging from the roof of the backstage dressing room. The staff were too late. No one previously knew that the two band members were homosexual. It's a tragedy and our condolences go out to all the families and fans of the two musicians. RIP.'

That troll-like stunt meant that the band's label had to shut down its site while the fake stories were removed. The Script didn't initially comment on the breach, but Danny later cheekily tweeted the title of their hit 'Dead Man Walking' in response to the pathetic prank. A few days later, however, he said, 'I'm supposed to be dead, but as you can hear, I'm really not. I had family and friends reading that – it was awful.'

As they got ready for their next landmark gig – headlining Oxegen – Danny recalled his first performance at the festival two years earlier, as he felt it was a turning point for the band. 'It was the middle of the day, it was a tough spot and we went out,' he told the *Irish Mirror*. 'I don't know what happened but it ended up being one of the finest gigs we ever played. I think we changed 80,000 people's minds all in 45 minutes. I could literally feel us turning the crowd, and here we are two years later on the main stage just ahead of the Black Eyed Peas.

'We did a long stint in the States – we were on tour for about six or seven weeks. You are in a country out of your own surroundings with different tea, different milk, different everything – everything about being on the road in America was different to what we were used to. It almost felt like The Script were in a battle to break America, as we aren't a homegrown act there. But everything that happened was amazing and we really felt we were back on the front line again.

'People would ask us if we weren't pissed off going back to 300-seater venues after supporting U2 and I would say no way. Because I know this is the start of what U2 did, and we were just as happy to get back on the trail and hopefully someday we will have the same success.

'There have been so many good moments – the second album going number one in the UK and Ireland was fantastic – the first album had that success but to achieve that on the second was unbelievable. And getting to see places like Manila. South Africa was our biggest indoor show – we did that in front of 18,000 people, which was incredible as we had never even been there before. We sold 10,000 for one show and 18,000 for the next, so there you go – there's an Irish band from James's Street playing to that many people. And now we are doing

Oxegen this weekend! That's the type of dream we are talking here.'

Their love of collaborating would continue too, writing songs with Tinie Tempah, who had supported them on some tour dates. And as if proof were needed of how hardworking the band are, particularly when it comes to cracking America, they signed up for a gig at the MGM Grand casino hotel in Las Vegas that October, and before it an even more unusual slot in New York, which they were able to schedule into their US tour. They were to perform at the New York State Fair in September where, because of the challenging economy, guests were to get a chance to see national acts without paying more than regular admission. The Script were in the line-up alongside Bruno Mars, country singers and celebrity chefs.

'Ten years of struggle, ten years of pushing, of people telling you, "You're too old" – it's all bollocks,' Danny told *Newsday* on his way to New Orleans in the middle of October. 'Here I am, I turned 30 and I'm sitting there laughing, laughing at everybody who said, "You're too old. You won't work with this demographic. You need to change this. You need to change that." I don't need to change!'

For Danny it was obvious that while they were huge in Europe and other countries, they had to downsize for the US, where despite chart success, filling arenas was still only a dream. 'To be honest, I'll play in your front room for a beer, you know? For me, it's a bittersweet thing,' he said. 'For all the success we've had in Europe, it's been a long, hard slog here in America. But it feels like this is the tour just before the tipping point ... it feels like we're back in the trenches again. We've got a good energy and we're not taking anything for granted.

'I wouldn't say we've arrived because there's still something that this band's gonna do that's going to change the course – I wouldn't say of music, I wouldn't be that brash – but it's going to change something and we just haven't done it yet.'

For lifelong Manchester United fan Danny, there was at least one perk to being famous – and he jumped at the chance to be at a special party celebrating Sir Alex Ferguson's managerial career. The band would perform and the stellar guest list included fellow Irishmen such as actor James Nesbitt, TV host Eamonn Holmes and sports stars such as golfer Rory McIlroy, rugby ace Brian O'Driscoll, jockey AP McCoy and former Red Devils heroes like Roy Keane.

'His son [Jason] asked us to play for the anniversary along with Mumford & Sons,' Danny told the *Sun* in December 2012. 'To be asked by the son of this absolute legend because we are one of his favourite bands was just bizarre. It was an amazing moment.

'Rio Ferdinand and I are pretty good mates. It's funny because I used to have all his jerseys and I asked him if he could sign one at Sir Alex's 25th anniversary. Rio said he was a big fan of our music and that he loved *The Voice*. We met up in London a few weeks later when he wasn't called up for England duty – shame on Hodgson, by the way – and had a few drinks. He's such a sound lad and the way he conducts himself on and off the pitch is very commendable.

'Someone else who I had a bit of a barney with was the legendary Norman Whiteside, over how many states there are in America. I said there were 52 and he said there were only 50. I thought I was so right that I bet £100 on it. Later, he emailed me saying that the two states I thought were in there, weren't. I had been so convinced and he ended up showing me that Norman has a lot more wisdom than Danny O'Donoghue!'

CHAPTER 11

DANNY FINDS HIS VOICE

In late 2011, Danny – with the backing of his band mates – made a move that would propel him and The Script to new heights. It was a clever and calculated move. He had been asked by the BBC if he would be interested in starring as a coach in the UK version of *The Voice*, a reality TV singing contest that had already proved a hit across the world but especially in the US, where Christina Aguilera and CeeLo Green were mentors.

The brainchild of John de Mol, the man behind *Big Brother*, the show begins with 'blind auditions', where the contestants sing and the four celebrity judges, sitting in huge red chairs, sit with their backs to them. If they like what they hear, they press their buzzers and the chair swings round. If more than one turns, the contestant has the chance to pick which one they want to coach them, until each coach has 10 acts.

Later stages of the contest see head-to-head sing-offs and then public votes, but the blind auditions are certainly the most exciting hook to the series. Unlike *The X Factor* and other shows, contestants on *The Voice* are judged first and foremost on their vocal ability, rather than their looks or stage performance.

He might have two No 1 albums under his belt, but Danny had the lowest profile of the four judges, by virtue of the fact that Tom Jones, Black Eyed Peas star will.i.am and Jessie J were the other coaches. And that was the reasoning behind his decision to sign up, as Mark explained: 'Danny did *The Voice* to put a face to The Script. We know about producing, songwriting and performing – we've been doing it since we were 14 or 15. Danny on a show about singing was good for us. People saw how passionate he is about music, how much it means to him and it made our band better known.'

The initial reaction saw cheap jibes directed at him on Twitter, with users branding him 'Danny I Dunno Who'. He soon won people over with his affable personality and cheeky Irish charm, but not before the 'I Dunno Who' gag was copied by critics in newspapers and, most notably, by comedian James Corden when he was hosting the 2012 BRIT Awards.

Danny retaliated with, 'James who? Whatever. It's up to other people to make up their own minds. I know I'm on this show for what I've done in my career. I've spent 15 years in the music industry, it's all I know.'

The 'I Dunno Who' jibe soon lost any potency; in fact

the band enjoyed the hoped-for boost in sales off the back of Danny appearing on *The Voice*.

In December 2011 the full line-up was finally announced for the show, which would launch on TV in March 2012 and be presented by Holly Willoughby and Reggie Yates. In February 2012 *Broadcast* magazine said the show was 'rumoured to have cost the corporation some £20m – and, as one of channel controller Danny Cohen's first major entertainment commissions, there is a lot riding on its success or failure.' Half a million pounds was spent on will.i.am's fee alone, according to *The Guardian*, with Sir Tom Jones taking home an estimated £250,000, Jessie J a little less, and Danny said to be pulling in six figures.

'I'm a massive fan of *The Voice*, so to be involved as a coach is amazing,' Danny declared in the press release. 'This is a show unlike any other because it puts vocal ability first above all else. I look forward to putting my team together and battling it out with the other coaches to see who wins this unique, credible competition. I'm in it to win it!'

Danny was seen as a surprise addition to the panel in some quarters, not least because it appeared he had snatched his place from Will Young, himself a reality TV winner on *Pop Idol*. Young had been an early contender for the role and had been in talks over the part before Danny was chosen at the eleventh hour and Young was left fuming. 'Words escape me,' he wrote on his Twitter page. 'Life is sometimes a bitch. *The Voice* came, *The*

Voice went. They wanted to go more rock ... Should have dusted off my leather jacket! Hey ho ... I'm holding a seance with Hendrix.'

'I'd planned it all: my clothing range and rise to A-list celebrity, my house in the Bahamas,' he told the *Daily Express*. 'I don't think I have ever been treated like that – been led on so long for a job and then had it taken away, or ever been so weirdly upset about it. It was a great reminder that this business is a cruel one.'

The subject quickly became a trending topic on Twitter, but BBC1 boss Cohen justified his decision, saying, 'Danny is a rising star who will bring freshness and surprise to the team.'

One suggestion was that Danny was preferred over Young as he offered greater sex appeal, but Danny told the *Irish Sun* that he found that strange. 'To hear that is so weird,' he said. 'We're not a band who's into that kind of thing. I mean, we've never even had our faces on the cover of our albums – we've never promoted ourselves in that way. I have a face for radio, so they may want to look to someone else on the show to bring the sex appeal; it's not me.'

'I'd interviewed for the position and been called back,' Danny added to the *Irish Daily Mail*, 'but I heard that people like Mary J Blige were also in the running. I knew Will Young was the favourite. As far as I was aware, there was a lot of hearsay and rumour and I didn't know anything for sure. But I was so thrilled to get the job.'

'I've got the gift of the gab, I guess,' he told the *Irish*

Sun. 'The Irish have it. We all went through the same screening process, I just managed to talk my way in.'

Stereophonics singer Kelly Jones later revealed that he too had been approached about the role that eventually went to Danny. 'Maybe I was a bit edgier,' Danny told *The Times*, but it helped that he also made the producers laugh with his cheeky charmer personality. 'I hadn't realised I'd spent the entire interview sitting on the pin of my BBC pass. I'd wondered what was hurting me so much.' After he got up and fixed himself, he turned round and cracked a joke about it. 'I'm sure that's why I got the job,' he says.

With the blessing of his band-mates, Danny threw himself into the new project. 'I'm sure people at home [in Ireland] are like, "Why the hell is he on the English show?"' he said to the *Irish Sun*. 'We all sat down and discussed whether this would be a good move for the band, and the pros and cons of doing the show, and came to the conclusion that it would be a great programme to be a part of and a great boost for the band itself. I'm not going solo: I'd be lost without Mark and Glen.'

There was plenty of hype surrounding the show before it aired and all four coaches announced themselves in style in the first episode by joining forces to sing the Black Eyed Peas hit 'I've Gotta Feeling', with Danny playing piano. The four quickly gelled, expressing mutual respect for each other. Will.i.am was impressed by Danny early on, saying, 'Danny from The Script is talented. A writer, singer and producer – he's dope.'

'I love Will,' Danny told the *Irish Sun*. 'I'm having a lot of fun working on the show with him and now we're looking at some tracks and there's definitely a standout or two that will be released. I don't know about doing that during the actual show itself – might be a bit desperate, if you ask me. Although, it didn't harm "Moves Like Jagger" for Adam Levine and Christina Aguilera.' In fact, the fruit of their collaboration was released as a single later in the year and it turned out to be the mega hit 'Hall of Fame'.

But it wasn't just will.i.am Danny bonded with. 'Jessie is this force of nature, and Tom is a legend – I'm learning so much from everyone,' he said. 'It's such a unique experience I never thought I'd get. I kind of feel like it's these three world-class legends on the coaching panel, then me. I don't really fit in, but I'm trying my best.'

Danny revealed that the four coaches had been quite guarded at first but got to know each other over drinks and dinner. 'That was just a real ice breaker for us,' he said. 'Tom Jones puts you at ease, telling some stories about him and Elvis or him and Van Morrison on a plane. When you find someone you love musically, it's hard not to get on like a house on fire. We all got there on our own merit. I respect that about them.'

He was also keen to make the most of his opportunities on the show and collaborate with the other two judges as well. 'I won't be going solo,' he said, 'but I'd be mad not to sit there and say to Tom, "Do you need a song or two?"'

By the end of February and with the blind auditions complete, Danny couldn't contain his excitement ahead of the live shows. 'I'm like a giddy kid,' he told *Daily Star Sunday*. 'The quality of talent on the show is unbelievable. There aren't any novelty acts. And there are lots of people who have auditioned who've said they wouldn't audition for *X Factor* for fear of being ridiculed.'

That rivalry with *The X Factor* was soon marked. Even though they did not clash in the schedules, the obvious comparisons and battle lines were drawn. Danny told the *Irish Sun* that he was more qualified than his Irish counterpart on *The X Factor*, Louis Walsh. 'I've way more to bring to the table,' he said. 'The one thing I've been saying since I got the job in *The Voice* is: "Please don't compare me to Louis."

'It's the Irish thing straight away, "Oh, you're the Louis Walsh of *The Voice*", just because we're from the same country, and I'm the only Irish person on the panel. I think some, let's say, less informed, folk assume we'll be similar. But there's a huge difference between us – it's like night and day. I'm in a band: I'm a singer. He's never been in a band and doesn't know that journey to get there. Yeah, he's got years of managing bands behind him and he's really excellent at what he does and knows his side of the business so well, but actually being in a band, actually performing on stage, that's what I'm bringing to the table.

'The differences are obvious … Managing bands is vastly different to being in one. I offer a raw approach. And for a show like this, I've a lot more to offer to singers looking to get a foothold in the industry. I've been there and I've had doors slammed in my face over and over when I first started out and that's the only way to learn how to make it, so I know what these guys are going through. And I think unless you've been on that journey, you can't really offer advice to anyone.'

They might not have been directly up against *The X Factor*, but *The Voice* would overlap with that other behemoth of Simon Cowell TV shows, *Britain's Got Talent*. The press were salivating as the two went head-to-head with some mudslinging between the respective stars of the shows.

Danny, given the show nickname 'Mr Hyper' behind-the-scenes, backed *The Voice* to win the head-to-head. 'The quality of everything is as good as it can be,' he told the *Daily Star Sunday*. 'No expense has been spared … from the set to all the production. I'm so confident, happy and excited about *The Voice* I don't think we need to worry about what other shows are doing.

'Tom Jones was telling a story about Frank Sinatra when he was a kid … Frank told Tom, "Put in some emotion but don't put too much emotion in because then you start to strain your voice," and Tom told that to this kid on the show. Tom Jones turned around and went, "That was from Frankie to me, from me to you."'

When it came to the blind auditions, Danny said they were full of surprises, including his mistaking a man for a woman on one occasion. 'I loved the voice and when I turned around I expected to see a woman there and it was a guy. That's the best thing about this show, the shocks. I have had people listen to my voice and not know who is singing and they have mistaken me for a woman. It's funny. Maybe it's all the hairspray.

'A voice can come from anywhere, from someone skinny, fat, small, tall. The big voices coming out of little people were amazing. That is the shock of *The Voice*, when you don't know what it is you will turn around to.'

Danny told the *Evening Times* that six-times Grammy and double Brit award winner Adele would have been rejected by Simon Cowell's show, but embraced by *The Voice*. 'We need to take the music industry by the scruff of the neck and get it back out of "everybody needs to be in this mould and if you're not in this silhouette of what a pop star should be, then you're not getting in." There are artists out there breaking the mould. Adele's a perfect example.'

Ahead of the anticipated ratings battle between *The Voice* and *Britain's Got Talent,* Danny explained why he signed up to *The Voice* when he had never been a fan of TV singing contests.

'The reason I was so anti-talent shows in the past was because of the way they were painting people,' he told the *Irish Daily Mail*. 'I have worked in a TV company before and I know how you can edit and manipulate a certain situation to make it go a certain way. And I watch it and I see that it does go on for other shows: people's words getting cut off halfway through. But I can honestly put my hand on my heart and say I knew it was something different.

'It was putting the power of musicianship back into musos' hands. We had seen 110 people over the course of three days. And I was asking them why *The Voice*? And they said to me it was because of the blind auditions. You are going to sing for four people and all you will be judged on is your voice. Not your looks, not your background and that says it all.'

Danny quickly enjoyed blossoming relationships with his co-stars. Jessie J said she was 'like a sponge' absorbing the experience of her co-stars and she also ended up collaborating with Danny. 'Danny is someone who is a vocalist and a songwriter,' she said. 'I've been helping him with vocals and he's been helping me with songwriting and we've been at the piano.'

Danny said he learnt a new trick from Jessie as well! 'Jessie taught me how to get liquid in your mouth when there's no water around,' he revealed. 'It's about rolling your tongue around your lips. She looks great doing it. I kept asking her to show me how to do it.'

Danny described Jessie J as an 'understated artist' and Black Eyed Peas star will.i.am as 'more than a musician', but it was clear that he bonded with fellow Celt and elder statesman Tom Jones the most. He and Tom shared the biggest laughs, with the crooner leaving him in stitches all day.

'He is always winding me up,' Danny told the *Irish Daily Mail*. 'If we are both bidding for the one singer, he is always saying: "Never trust the Irish" and I have to hit back with "The Welsh are just the Irish that couldn't swim."'

The pair would also share a drink and some banter after the cameras stopped rolling. 'We drink into the early hours of the morning,' said Danny. 'It's not me drinking him under the table – it's the other way round. He can hold his own. We have a right laugh together.'

At the same time Danny, Mark and Glen were working on The Script's third album during Danny's downtime from the show. With Danny's profile raised due to *The Voice*, the pressure was on to produce a stellar record to seize the moment. 'This third album is going to be crucial for us, a real pinnacle album and could set us up for the next five to ten years as to what sort of a band we will be perceived as,' said Danny. 'We are really trying to make an effort to get our music out to as many people as possible.'

The extra workload was no problem for Danny and he had the full support of Mark and Glen. 'They are massive fans of the show too,' he told the *Daily Mirror*. 'This year is going to be packed, but what I love is the fact that 2012 is all about music. I wouldn't like to be on a TV show that was talking about something like gardening, for instance. I want to give *The Voice* everything – and I have to say that I really am enjoying every aspect of the show so far.'

The show's co-presenter Reggie Yates felt that everyone was getting on really well and that 'everyone falls in love with Danny'. Yet Danny gave some fighting talk to the *Daily Mirror* on 15 March ahead of the show's opening night: 'Even on the first day of auditions, the talent on it beat any final I have ever seen on a talent contest. The standard was just incredible,' he said. 'I have always been a massive fan of the US show. I fell in love with the format and the fact that the coaches cannot see the people singing. So many of my friends would have liked to have gone on a singing talent TV show in the past, but they didn't for fear of being ridiculed. It is fantastic that *The Voice* is all about finding fantastic singers.

'Look, I have been in the music business since I was 16. I know exactly what it is like and I can give them so much help and advice on what to do and look out for. I do have a raw view of the industry. I think I have built up a vast amount of experience in all things music and I've done everything from producing to owning a mini record label and starting The Script. I want to teach some of the things I have learned along the way to my own group and tell them the best way to go about their careers.'

With four powerful egos vying for attention, there were bound to be arguments and heated moments. 'There were loads of bust-ups,' revealed Danny. 'We are all very competitive. I couldn't say who is the most competitive, probably either Will or Jessie.'

Despite his burgeoning status as a pin-up, Danny told the *Sun* that he would have been rejected by normal TV talent shows because of the way he looked. 'There are a lot of people out there who you take a look at and think they are not a pop star, but then you hear them sing and they are incredible. Look at Adele. I am not a normal pop star either.

'On *The Voice*, we are giving it back to those musicians

and those singers who thought they were overweight or over the hill. This show is here to find artists who have a voice and who are willing to go the extra mile. I've picked my team on their voice alone – and I hope once the public starts voting in the live shows, they will have fallen in love with their voice, too.

'Why would I want to change anyone? I have never been asked to change myself and I wouldn't want that with my team either. The talent on the show has blown me away and I really do think I have found three or four people who have a good shot at the title. I am over the moon with my choices for my team.'

Danny told the paper that he hoped his team would heed his advice and learn from his experience, but added that he was not going to wrap them up in cotton wool either. 'They are all accomplished singers and they have already been through the mill, so I want to train them on performing to bring out the best in them. Everyone is their own person. Once you put the shackles on them, they break free even more. But if someone has a bad time, I am definitely there to offer a shoulder to cry on.'

Danny revealed to the *Sun* how he and Sir Tom had already formed an unlikely 'bromance' by going out for a few pints. 'Tom has come from an era which is awesome. His background is very similar to my own and I love listening to all his stories. I get on well with Tom and we have shared a few drinks. In fact, the first night we all went out together as coaches, Jessie and Will headed back to the studio while Tom and I stayed out until 1am.'

But he also insisted that while he enjoys a drink and smoke, he is smart enough to know all about the dangers of excess and not succumbing to the darker side of celebrity, where drugs have ruined the lives of so many talented music stars.

'I do and I don't enjoy myself,' he told the *Sun*. 'When the time is right I do. But there are too many people out there who have taken it to excess. We've had Amy Winehouse, Pete Doherty, Whitney Houston. People know the pitfalls of rock 'n' roll and they know what it does to you. But people are still doing it and I do think it is down to the individual.'

Danny told *Metro* that he had one key piece of advice for his charges: be nice to people. 'Treat people from the porter on the way into the studio to the producer on the way out nicely and with respect. Life's one big revolving door – you never know who is going to be helping you in one way and kicking you out the other side. You don't have to be an arsehole to make it in the music industry – it's not a prerequisite.'

Ahead of the first episode, Danny appeared on the *Capital Breakfast Show* with Dave Berry and Lisa Snowdon and reinforced his message. 'My acts are going to be thrust into the limelight and they need to learn how to be gracious and shake everyone's hands – because the runners of today are the producers of tomorrow. We need to teach people manners.'

That said, he confessed that his main worry was accidentally swearing on the show. 'I tend to curse a lot,' he admitted, 'so God forgive me when we get to the live shows. I'm in training now for the next seven weeks to not curse on the live shows. I'm very passionate and I have a limited dictionary to express myself with.'

In the event, *The Voice* claimed first blood in the ratings war with *Britain's Got Talent* when the two shows overlapped for 20 minutes on the first night, with 8.9 million viewers to 6.6 million. Even Simon Cowell congratulated the BBC.

Danny came clean to the *Irish Mirror* that he had to wear make-up on the show, making light of the whole thing but also his point at the end. 'I could say I don't want make-up, but then I'd end up looking like a corpse,' he told the newspaper. 'So I sit there and they put a bit of whatever on, but no false eyelashes yet. I've been making a real effort to pick out my clothes in the morning and to find matching socks. I'm so Hollywood, aren't I?

'It isn't *Britain's Next Top Model*. You can look at who you want, but at the end of the day you're going to have to listen to me too.'

The show turned Danny into an instant sex symbol and sent the Twittersphere into meltdown. One fan tweeted: 'Good god if I didn't fancy #dannyodonoghue before I definitely do now #idlovemeanirishman' and another wrote: 'dannyodonoghue is my new love!'

His raised profile also meant that Danny was getting propositioned left, right and centre by even more women than before, but he still only had eyes for Irma. 'Yeah, there's some crazy stuff that comes in on Twitter and that,' he told the *Sun* on 5 April. 'I get things like, "Show me yours and I'll show you mine". I'm like, "No!" But at least I know there are offers if I'm ever down on my luck.'

Danny was upfront and honest when he signed up for *The Voice* – it was essentially to raise his profile and, in turn, benefit The Script. The money was good too: he was reported to be getting £100,000 a series. While this was the lowest of fee of the four judges, it was still a significant sum of cash. But it was the boost for the band that he was more interested in – and it didn't take long in coming. After the show first aired, five Script singles re-entered the charts, and their two albums were selling 6,000 copies a week. *The Daily Telegraph* reported that after two episodes, record sales for all the coaches were booming and The Script's debut album was back in the Top 10 – four years after its release!

Danny told his 101,000 Twitter followers at the time: 'Another 20 thousand followers album is at 5 and the second album at 20. This is just stupid now !!!;)'

On 9 April *Billboard* reported that not only were The Script's albums back in the American charts, but their 2008 No 2 hit 'The Man Who Can't Be Moved' had jumped from number 61 to number 18.

Not everybody was happy with the commercial aspect of the show. On 3 April the *Daily Mail* headline asked: Is THE BBC'S *THE VOICE* JUST A BIG ADVERT? MP QUESTIONS SHOWS PROMOTION OF RECORD LABEL. Conservative MP Philip Davies wasn't happy that the BBC had shelled out £22 million to secure *The Voice*, yet three of the four coaches (everyone but Danny) were signed to Universal, with the contest winner getting signed to the record label and the runners-up being signed to a subsidiary.

Davies, who sits on the Media Select Committee, said: 'The BBC has paid a fortune for *The Voice*. This now looks to be a very expensive advert for the record company which not only gets a heavily promoted winner but also a boost for its existing artists on the show. The BBC also appears to be using this format as a spoiler to sabotage ITV's success with *Britain's Got Talent*. On both of these counts I don't think this is what the BBC should be doing.'

The BBC responded: '*The Voice* is an established global format with pre-existing arrangements. In addition to the usual strict editorial measures, the BBC have taken appropriate steps to ensure there can be no editorial influence [by Universal]. In casting the coaches, we spoke to the biggest stars in the music industry regardless of the labels they were attached to.'

Danny and Jessie J showed they had no problems taking the gloves off when they clashed over contestant Cassius Henry. As Jessie tried to woo him, she took a pop at Danny's dress sense: 'Don't trust people who wear denim on denim!' Sharp as a tack, Danny retorted: 'I say never trust a girl who wears so much bling but sings about not worrying about the price tag.'

Danny was moved emotionally when he heard one contestant, David Julien, sing a Script song. 'There was a guy who sang "The Man Who Can't Be Moved" and I felt the same emotion hearing him sing as when I wrote the song and I turned around,' he told the *Daily Star* on 24 March. 'I couldn't not turn around, you know? The guy actually quit his job stacking shelves on the morning of the audition to be on the show. That's what I would have done.'

Danny told the former Sainsbury's worker on the show: 'I have to tell you, man, you've got some *cojones* coming out here and singing my song! We belong together.'

Welsh student Hannah Berney even picked Danny ahead of fellow countryman Tom Jones after Danny told her: 'I see from the tears on your face that this means a lot to you.'

But there was a more significant auditionee in this episode of *The Voice*, one who would have a profound impact on Danny – Lady Catherine Anna Brudenell-Bruce, daughter of the Earl of Cardigan, or Bo Bruce, as she announced herself on the show. Posh she might have been, but she also came with a certain amount of baggage. After an an unhappy childhood she had become estranged from her father, even taking out a restraining order against him, and had successfully battled drink and drug abuse. On her website she said her life had been 'a spiralling mess of drugs and alcohol' before she'd gone into rehab. She also had to cope with her mum Ros's fight with pancreatic cancer during filming for the show.

On the 14 April episode it was Danny and will.i.am who had the bitchy bust-up, over accusations of copying as they spun round for the same artists on a number of occasions. 'There is a bit of rivalry between me and Will,' Danny said. 'We tend to turn on the same people. As soon as I turn around, oh, he is already there. I guess it still remains to be seen who is actually copying who. Every time I turned around, he was there.'

Will.i.am hit back: 'We know damn well I wasn't following his button-pushing. That's his tactics. I don't have tactics. I've got Tic Tacs because I stay fresh.'

One contestant – Jenny – opted for will.i.am over Danny, purely because she had such a crush on The Script frontman. 'I chose Will over Danny because I really fancy Danny and wouldn't have been able to work with him!' she admitted.

He was, indeed, becoming the show's resident sex symbol. The *Sun*'s *Fabulous* magazine ran a special feature and photoshoot with him with the headline: 'Danny cool – he's the man who's made Saturday nights worth staying in for. Say hello to Danny O'Dono-phew, TV's hottest new star, in more ways than one!'

'After the first show went out I had 200 marriage proposals in two days,' Danny told the mag. 'Crazy stuff. And I get a lot of girls tweeting the same message over and over asking me to follow them, which is a bit like someone constantly ringing your doorbell,' he says. 'I'm loving it though. I see it as a bit of fun unless it starts getting stalkerish. My mother checks my Twitter, and I wouldn't like her to see what people have said they'd like to do to me.'

But it was water off a duck's back for Danny, who

admitted that he was quite used to attracting the attention of adoring females. 'Yeah, it can be quite distracting when I'm singing something heartfelt about the breakdown of a relationship like our single "Breakeven", and there's some girl in the front row making, well, obscene gestures with her mouth.'

But he was still very much in love with Irma and brushed aside the notion that he would ever stray. 'I'd be more worried about her getting chatted up than me,' he said. 'Every relationship has to start with trust. When I was younger and didn't know what love was, then things were different. But now, I'm absolutely a one-woman man.

'I look for confidence in a partner. I like girls who are up for a challenge. Someone to go walking and hill climbing with and who doesn't mind trawling through the shit across fields. Someone who likes to get their hands dirty. Looks can matter, but someone doesn't have to be extremely attractive for you to fall in love with them. It's the personality that makes a girl gorgeous. Mind, if she's beautiful too then you've got a winning package.'

But his raised profile now meant that he attracted much more attention in public. 'Yeah I suppose I am a beacon of recognisability – 6ft 4in, tattoos and big hair,' he says. 'It's only a few weeks in and I can't walk down the street any more. Coffee shops completely stop if I'm walking by. So I know life is going to be different.'

Different yes, in terms of being recognised, but on a personal level nothing had changed. Danny was still living in the same suburban bedsit he'd been renting since he'd first moved to London four years earlier. And he didn't have a driving licence so there would be no flash sports car parked outside either.

'Even though we've achieved all that with The Script, my mum's only pleased now that I'm working for the BBC because it's a job with some security. The bedsit I use as a place to crash more than anything. I occasionally start looking at apartments on the laptop, but then get distracted by something else that drags me away from it. And what's the point of earning a shitload of money to go and blow it on a Ferrari? I'm not going to drive down to Sainsbury's or go to the beach with my mates in that, am I?'

By the 14 April show, *The Voice* was hitting 12.2 million viewers – twice as many as *Britain's Got Talent*. By this stage Danny had his 10 acts – Max Milner, Aleks Josh, Emmy J Mac, John James Newman, Vince Freeman, Murray Hockridge, Hannah Berney, David Julien, Bill Downs and Bo Bruce – and had been given singer Paloma Faith to assist him in coaching them.

'I hadn't met Danny before but he is such a lovely person,' said Paloma afterwards. 'He is a carer and he has invested a lot in his team.'

'I have 10 children plonked on my doorstep at the one time,' said Danny. 'It really feels like that, like their lives and careers are in my hands. It feels like I owe them everything and they'll definitely get it from me.'

On 20 April, Danny told the *Daily Mirror* how his life had changed in a matter of weeks, thanks to *The Voice*'s many millions of viewers and associated radio, press and magazine coverage. Now he was getting mobbed in the street everywhere he went.

'It's mad,' said Danny. 'I've had more than 300 marriage proposals now. I kept showing people my Twitter and it was another one, another one, they kept coming. Things have changed. People think they know you and say "hi" in the chipper and the street. Then they realise they don't know you. They just know you from TV. It is big, like hold on to your fucking hats. It is a bigger, broader reach and now I am Danny from *The Voice*, not Danny from The Script. I love it.'

Another love throughout this time would be his photography – Irma would even let him do photoshoots with her model pals. 'I am really into photography, the lighting and everything. I have a camera with me all the time. I have the last three years of my life with The Script on hard drives in photos, I haven't got a great memory, but now I have got all my memories in HD. It is brilliant.'

As the acts were whittled down, some of his team took defeat better than others. Bill Downs, who had postponed his wedding after Danny picked him, lost out and was gutted. Vince Freeman took his axing even harder, refusing to shake Danny's hand after he had chosen Bo Bruce ahead of him for the live shows. 'I am livid about it,' he said after the show.

For all the hurt involved for the hopefuls, Danny told

the *Telegraph Online* that he would have gone on *The Voice* if it had existed when he was young. 'Without a shadow of a doubt. I don't want to get into a war with anyone but there was a certain amount of musicality missing from the acts and judging of other TV talent shows. Most of the artists on *The Voice* piss all over the UK pop scene. You've got kids being kicked off our show who are actually better singers than I am, and I'm supposed to be judging! I just hope fans go, "Where the heck have all these people been?" Seriously. Why are we watching R&B singers out of breath and miming on Saturday morning TV? It should give the whole UK industry a kick up the ass.

'I've been giving my tuppence worth of advice all along in my career, which generally falls on deaf ears. I've been a songwriter, musician, producer, had two record deals, been a massive failure, clawed my way out to be in a successful band. I've dealt with nerves, bad performances, feeling defeated. I wish I knew all this stuff when I was 17 and standing backstage waiting to go on TV and make a show of myself. I do feel I have things to pass on to other artists.'

Danny said that it had been the harsh moment when cameras had caught him as Brit awards host James Corden referred to him as 'Danny I Dunno Who?' that the penny had dropped. He and the band realised they had to start raising their profile and getting proper credit for their work.

'It was one of those moments when I went: "Wow,

nobody has a clue who we are as a band,"' he said. 'We are faceless, the non-toast of the town. So I got an opportunity to go on TV and get our personality and ethos across, show where our music comes from, because I believe our songs have meaning and purpose, and I'd like everyone in the world to hear a Script song at least once. Is that wrong?

'It's not about the money,' he insisted. 'I still live in the same flat I was in when we first released an album. If you gave me a million dollars and said: "What do you want to do?" – I'm already doing it! This is what I want!

'The hardest part is the delivery of the decision, not the decision itself, which, honestly, might be made before. It's to do with focus, personality, talent, creativity and drive to make it past the show. [My artists] Max, Bo, Hannah, Alex, David all play guitar and write their own songs. I'm trying to get them ready, so that when they reach the market place, they just float.

'Some people might think I'm the underdog, but the BBC have told me I am the most organised of all the judges. I make it my business to know this stuff. When they're done with me, they're going to be able to walk through the industry with their heads held high.'

Danny also told the *Sun* that the quality of the singing was so good that it made him feel almost like a fraud. 'I promise that on some occasions, someone would open his or her mouth and I'd be thinking, "You're better than me. How on earth am I going to give you pointers?" But mentoring isn't about teaching them to sing, it's about bringing out the best version of themselves.

'I've tasted failure and come out the other side. I got a second chance. It's set me up well to help the members of Team Danny. Shows like this change the game in TV, bringing families back together around the box. It offers a real window into the industry and to artists in different stages of their career.'

Danny told *Daily Star Sunday*, 'This year's talent has been amazing but I think next year's show will be tenfold. You are going to get lots of talented artists who would never have dreamed of auditioning before, coming to *The Voice*. I was on radio with *Britain's Got Talent* [*BGT*] winner Jai McDowall and even he admitted that he would have preferred to audition for *The Voice*. That speaks volumes. *The Voice* has elevated the level of talent people expect to see now. It's another level to *BGT* and *The X Factor*. You don't have to be cruel for ratings. And I think *The Voice* ratings speak for themselves.'

He told the *Sun*, 'The stance we've taken is that you can deliver bad news in a good way,' he explained. 'Maybe it's not great for ratings but we had a 17-year-old on our show and she wasn't great. Are we going to destroy her so she couldn't walk down the street? Absolutely not. You could have ruined her life if you did to her what other reality shows have done to people.

'If you take this to the schoolyard, what would you say to your kids if they were like "Off, off, off" to a five-year-old? I'm not there to say, "You're shit, get off!" I give them constructive criticism. I know it doesn't make for good TV [but] I don't want to bring people to tears. Who wants to see a kid cry? We've been there, been told we're crap or whatever. Other talent show judges that haven't can be more catty.

'I'm sure on other shows they all sit back and watch the VTs [video tapes] about what's going on that day and decide in the room what to say beforehand,' he said. 'We don't. We made a clear decision that the reactions you see are instant ones. I won't play up [to the cameras]. That's not what music is about. Music isn't a pantomime.

'Simon Cowell said he feared for his own shows because you have to turn out a star for your brand. Turning out a star worries me. I think our third, fourth, fifth-placed acts will all sell 100,000 or 120,000 records which in this day for a first album is astonishing. With the hits my team are getting online and on YouTube, if you switch that to sales and every click was a sale, they'd be sitting on £800,000 right now.'

Danny was spending 11 hours a day working with his acts. 'I don't think the BBC knew what they were letting themselves in for when they took me. I like to get involved in everything: how they crop the shots in the editing suite, styling, everything. I work really long hours. It's four days a week now, from 8am to 7pm. I try to give them as much advice as possible. I really want one of my team to win.

'I don't have a right to tell my team how to be likeable. I'm not that liked. But I can say to just be honest – don't stand looking at your shoes, being nervous. There's a big audience out there. We've experienced nervousness even in our own band. If you don't connect with people back home you're losing out.'

The people back home also wanted to connect with Danny, and in ever increasing numbers. 'Since the show started I'm relatively housebound,' he told *RTE Guide*. 'There are not many places I can go any more. It's crazy. People have tweeted me to say they had a dream the night before that they were on *The Voice*, or the next tweet is "Marry me, marry me!" It's surreal. Babies – those that can talk – shout "Telly! Man from the telly" when they see me.'

Poor Danny – he couldn't even be himself when recording the programme he loved so much. 'I get warned every show, "Please no cursing. We know you're Irish and it's part of your literature but please don't curse." So what I do is get it all out straight away – effin' and blindin' in the morning time and then when the show goes live, I'm fine. I was the only one when I went on *Loose Women* who was made to sign a contract saying I wouldn't swear. When you're on the BBC you're obviously impression-able, especially to young girls.'

It wasn't just his language he had to watch – it was ogling host Holly Willoughby, who often wore outfits with plunging necklines. 'Holly's boobs are amazing,' he confessed to the *Sun*. 'The last show I did get distracted. Me and Tom Jones both did. Tom said, "I want you on my team." And I told him, "That's not a contestant you're looking at." We want her on both our teams.'

Danny maintained to *The Observer* that starring on the

show had not elevated him to any sort of coolness – 'Bono or Sting – they're cool. Listen, nobody gives Bono the plaudits he deserves … Sting, he talks about feelings and emotions' – but it had won him even more fans.

'In four weeks I've got over 300,000 followers,' he said. 'Every second one is "Danny, will you marry me?" or "Danny, I had a dream about you last night." It's really confusing. What do you do with that? They all know I have a girlfriend. I think it's just an outpouring of affection. I think I come across as loving music to the core.'

But it all railed against The Script's approach: 'Never to put ourselves on poster campaigns or album covers. We don't want to be all about a look. It's just about the music. A lot of new music is light entertainment. I'd rather listen to Dylan because he tells me something about myself, but I see there's a below-20 age group that doesn't want to be singing about my dead father. It's an undeniable platform. You'd be stupid to think this isn't a great way of showcasing talent. All of my acts I'd work with outside this. They are such nice and talented people.'

Bo was Danny's choice for the final up against Tyler James (will.i.am), Vince Kidd (Jessie) and Leanne Mitchell (Tom Jones). But Danny was careful not to ask too much of her, because she was also trying to spend time with her terminally ill mum. 'Bo's got a massive chance to make it,' he told the *Sun*. 'Her mum has decided to move home from hospital so she can watch Bo in the final this weekend. I know how precious their time is together so I don't want to bring her to too much.'

He did take Bo busking and to some awards shows to help her profile ahead of the final and admitted he was in awe of her singing talent. 'The competition so far has been immense. There's been singers genuinely technically more gifted than myself, Jessie, Tom and Will up there that aren't on the show any more. I guess it goes past the voice itself: there's people who are technically gifted, and there's other people who sing from the heart, sing from the soul.

'Bo is one of those people. You don't have to sing every note that was ever invented to get your point across or sing a great song. And that's what the UK seems to be really, really responding to in Bo right now – the fact that she's willing to bare her soul on television in front of millions and millions of people. It's very rare.'

Come the final in June, Danny was in combative mood. 'I may have been the underdog at the start, but I feel more like a Rottweiler now,' he roared before the show. 'Twist me the wrong way and you'll see the Fighting Irish in me. It would be the upset of the century if Team Danny won the final, but Brits love a rags-to-riches story so don't count me out.

'Of course I want to beat them,' he added. 'We all have our egos and none of us likes to lose. You've already seen things get feisty between me and Will. It's not staged – we're both up there fighting for what we believe in. *The Voice* has changed my life.

'It will be absolutely spectacular. Take the winner of any singing talent show anywhere in the world, put them on a stage with any of our finalists and I bet they couldn't hold a candle to our guys.'

Bo, who sang Sinéad O'Connor's 'Nothing Compares 2 U' and performed Professor Green's 'Read All About It' as a duet with Danny, went into the final as favourite but it was to no avail as Leanne Mitchell, Tom Jones's act, was the unlikely winner.

The shock result might have explained why *The Voice* tour was then soon cancelled due to poor ticket sales.

Looking back, Jessie J, in her mini-autobiography *Nice To Meet You*, said of Danny: 'I'd always liked The Script's music, so I was looking forward to meeting Danny. He's pretty much exactly what you see on TV. He is the sweetest guy and he's very funny. He laughs at his own jokes! He's really honest, he has a big heart and he loves to learn. He's so interested in people and music and who's doing what. He loved doing *The Voice*. I'd be very surprised if Danny didn't come back for a second series. He bought me nail jewellery. So sweet.'

But Danny didn't take on the high-profile job to become famous in his own right – it was to promote The Script and his music style. 'It is a constant battle because it is a contradiction in a way, because yes, we actually are famous,' he told the *Irish Mail on Sunday*.

'People ask me why did I do *The Voice*? Well, if you look at today's industry there's a quarter of that show that they were going to give to either a [solo] musician or a reality TV star, Will Young. Or ... give it to the guy in a band, me. So, Mark was like, "Get in there for the band." There isn't much room for bands on the radio these days and it was all about putting The Script out there. And I managed to get our style of music represented on a show that teaches about music.'

The Script did receive a significant boost in their album sales from Danny's appearance on the series. On the flip side came a wave of media interest in his personal life, as a growing army of female fans clamoured to discover more about the strapping Irishman.

'It was LA Reid who warned me about that,' he says. 'He is our label boss in America and he told me to be prepared. Everything in your private life is going to get turned upside down. And I was like, "No man, you are crazy. Sure we can walk around Ireland and nobody hassles you." But it's a whole other thing in the UK. There used to be girls hanging around outside the house. Now it is old men in trench coats with cameras. And that is really hard to deal with.'

But, seeing the funny side as always, he adds, 'The amount of knickers I've been sent have reached Tom Jones levels! And it's a nice feeling having everyone wanting to shake my hand.'

The show did cause some moments of friction for the band as well, as when the band almost missed a sold-out date in Dubai when the BBC refused to release Danny from filming *The Voice*.

'They held him up and we'd to do a gig in Dubai that

Friday,' Mark revealed. 'They had a 16-seat private jet waiting for us at the airport, but still Danny wasn't let go. So myself and Glen flew out ahead of him. I wouldn't take the private plane anyway since I'm terrified of it. I flew out commercial, thinking Danny would soon follow.

'When it got to the afternoon of the show and he still hadn't left, we began to panic. Glen and I did the soundcheck on our own, which was weird. Then, all we could do was wait and see. When Danny got out, they'd swapped his plane for a tiny six-seater and he's so tall the eight-hour flight was very uncomfortable. They had to stop in Jordan to refuel – he made it with minutes to spare. He was in bits. It's the closest we've come to having to cancel a gig.'

The incident did strain relations with the BBC but the bottom line was that it was worth it. Going on the show achieved what he had set out to do, which was raise his profile and that of The Script. 'There's no programme to promote music on,' Danny says, 'not if you are a band. We're not edgy enough for Jools Holland but there are lots of great bands out there and it's a struggle.'

His point was proven practically overnight after appearing on *The Voice*, with his Twitter followers rocketing to thousands. 'I had to turn off my phone,' he said. 'It was a constant stream of messages, marriage proposals and nonsense. But I'm being mobbed for the right reasons – right now there's a big outpouring of love for The Script. It could have gone the other way. You never know what way I could have come across on television.'

CHAPTER 12

IT'S ALL OVER
WITH IRMA

Raw emotions such as heartache and pain fuel much of The Script's music. It's what draws so many fans to them, as they can identify with their lyrics. Danny would not have to look far for inspiration for his next album – he was left heartbroken when he and Irma split after four years together.

The Voice had only just finished in June 2012 when the press got wind of the break-up. Given the rumours and links to Bo Bruce, Danny's finalist on the show, the gossip mags and showbiz columns were ready to put two and two together – and get five.

Had their relationship been going in 'different directions' as the tabloids claimed, backed up by quotes from 'insiders'? Yes, Irma was based in Dublin – her career and more importantly her daughter were there.

Yes, Danny was based in London to film *The Voice*, but he'd had a bedsit base there for years before the TV show and it's a short hop from Dublin. He'd also spent the best part of the past four years either touring the world or recording music, so if they could make their relationship work around that, you wouldn't think that his career and being on *The Voice* was the reason for the split, as the *Irish Mirror* claimed on 6 June.

Rumours that the relationship was over began when Irma failed to turn up, as she had done for previous live shows, to support Danny at the final of *The Voice* in London. It would be a further two months before Danny broke his silence over the break-up, in a series of interviews after inviting the Irish press to Windmill Lane Studios in Dublin on 2 August for an exclusive preview session of their new album, #3.

Naturally it was the story of his split from Irma that dominated the interview questions – and the headlines the next day. 'It was just two people who weren't meant to be together,' he told the *Irish Mirror*. 'As much as things kind of play out in a relationship, I am going off in one way and you grow apart – not due to not liking each other or not loving each other but that happens sometimes. It happens to everybody and rather than me sitting here and saying it was her fault or my fault, we genuinely had a really great, amicable split. I wish her nothing but the best, she wishes me nothing but the best and it's just one of those things. It's, "Right I really appreciate the time I had with you and I love you to bits but it's not working out." And that's what happened.'

Danny also revealed that he had already channelled his heartache into a song for the new album, writing 'Six Degrees of Separation' with Mark about his relationship breakdown. Writing has always been a coping mechanism for Danny throughout the lows in his life, and this song would be his way of getting closure on the split. But he admitted he was also nervous about how it would be received by Irma.

'For us it is always about being personal,' he explained to the newspaper. 'It is the only way I believe you can get people emotionally involved in your music. And I think people see a certain sense of honesty and a certain sense of willingness to put your own neck out there and put your heart out to be slapped. It is a bit strange because with "The Man Who Can't Be Moved" it was a similar scenario.

'I never thought ... and only as you are saying it to me now I'm thinking, "Fuck, yeah, she is going to hear this." There are going to be consequences and now everything is going to be in the press. But the relationship we had, I think it would be foolish not to solidify that in a way and put that into musical form.

'It made its way out and obviously it meant that much to me that it has made its way and that is a testament as well. And it's not for any other reason than that's what is going on in my life. I would be foolish not to admit that "Six Degrees of Separation" was about me.'

Danny told the *Irish Sun* that it was his decision to call the relationship off – and it was the hardest thing he had ever done. 'Of course, it's the hardest fucking thing I've done in my life,' he said, before adding that he felt he had no choice but to write a song about his heartache. 'I very much wear my heart on my sleeve,' he said. 'If you're a good lead singer, you have to go out on a limb. A by-product of art is to be as honest and as truthful as you can.'

He told the *Irish Daily Mail* that despite the split, there still remained a love between the pair of them, so much so that parting was a grieving process. 'It was just that after four years together it had just run its course and that was that. And it was heart-breaking and upsetting and we had to grieve. But we still love each other – we'd just got to the place where we knew it wasn't going to work.'

Singing about the break-up in 'Six Degrees of Separation', while giving him closure, was at times upsetting as he remembered the love they shared. 'It's about those six stages you have to go through when you break up with someone,' he said. 'I think that anyone who has gone through a painful break-up will get that from the song. Irma knows about it and that's fine because it is art and not meant to upset anyone.'

As she moved on from the split, Irma looked forward to a new chapter in her life. She dyed her hair blonde and tried to focus on her aspirations to be an actress, winning a small role in the critically acclaimed crime drama *The*

Fall, a joint production between BBC and RTE starring Gillian Anderson and Jamie Dornan.

She gave her first interview to the *Irish Mail on Sunday* at the end of October and immediately laughed off any suggestions that she was upset that Danny had written a song about their relationship and break-up. 'This? This is nothing,' she said. 'To be honest, I laughed when I read the stories about us – so many of them were lies. I showed them to my mother and we laughed together about them. There are much more important things in life than all that.

'What was hard was reading about Nikoleta's father [Marius Simanaitis] when he passed away years ago,' she told the newspaper. 'There were so many untrue stories out there.

'Nikoleta is the most important thing in my life. Every day I take her to school, I collect her, I bring her to gymnastics, to dancing ... She's so determined and she loves performing. She is the best thing that has happened in my life. I think everything happens for a reason and I'm glad of everything I've gone through. I am so happy right now. I'm feeling very positive, I'm happy, I'm in a great place.'

It was being stung by stories in the tabloid media that had stopped Irma doing an interview before, and saw her turn down lucrative deals from magazines in Britain to kiss and tell about her love for, and split from, Danny. 'There were a lot of offers but I said, "No." I really don't think my life is that interesting and I don't have much to say. I love talking about my acting career and I'm happy to do that. But people always want something else. I'm not like that. I'm all about my job ... about modelling and acting. I keep my personal life to myself. I'm happy just to do my job and do it well.'

Irma had landed her first lead role, in a short film, *Normal*, which was all the more impressive when you remember she had arrived in Ireland just eight years previously, unable to speak a word of English. 'I knew nothing. I couldn't even go to the shop and ask for milk. I was struggling. I was here with a newborn baby and I couldn't speak the language.

'I remember the day I walked into First Options Modelling agency. Everyone had been saying I should try modelling and that I would be good. So I walked in there. All I could say was "Hello" and "Goodbye". But it was enough. I was so lucky and they signed me straight away. I've been working ever since.'

Two months later, on 12 December 2012, the second inquest into the death of Marius Simanaitis was heard – with the revelation that he had been playing with a weapon earlier in the evening. His death in 2009 had been the subject of an inquest at Dublin County Coroner's Court, where a verdict of suicide had been recorded but later quashed in the High Court following a judicial review sought by his brother Donatas.

At the new inquest, Dublin Coroner's Court heard that Marius had been drinking with friends at his apartment since about 6 pm the previous night. Lukas Tiskevirias said that Marius had been showing off the gun earlier in the evening before putting it away.

The *Irish Independent* reported that the inquest heard Marius had been talking about being 'cheated' out of a large sum of money which he was due to pass on to someone else and that his 'friends could not trust him any more,' he said.

That night, Marius had blocked the door of the apartment with a barbell, drawn the curtains and would not allow anyone to go onto the balcony. He had also been talking about his ex-partner Irma and their child. The last time Tiskevirias saw Marius, he was sitting with his head in his hands.

Tiskevirias told the court he was lying on the couch with his eyes closed at around 6 am when he heard a scratching noise. He then heard a shot and someone falling to the ground. When he opened his eyes, he saw Marius on the ground with a pool of blood around him.

Vilius Muznikas, who was also present, said he had witnessed Marius pick up and 'play' with the gun. 'He was clicking the top part and taking in and out the part where the bullets were. I told him not to play with the gun – it was dangerous and he could shoot me or my girlfriend.'

The couple went to bed and were woken up by Mr Tiskevirias, who was screaming, having discovered Mr Simanaitis.

When Irish police searched the apartment they found a kilogram of cannabis in Marius' bedroom.

Deputy state pathologist Dr Michael Curtis told the

court that death was due to a gunshot to the right of the head, in an area well recognised as a site used by people inflicting wounds on themselves. Dr Curtis said there was no evidence of assault. The toxicology report found Marius had been mildly intoxicated when he died and there was methamphetamine in his system. There was no evidence that Simanatis was murdered, the Dublin coroner found on the second day of the inquest. In summing up the case for the jury, Dr Farrell noted that the deceased's handling of the gun earlier in the night had caused some 'consternation' among those present and that he was intoxicated at the time of his death. The jury returned an open verdict.

All in all, it was a difficult year for Irma, and Danny too, but he was full of praise for the way Irma handled everything. 'She says they can say whatever they want,' he told the *Sun*'s *Fabulous* magazine. 'She's a very solid and good person. I'm sure it affects her though. I do still wear her ring, but I suppose I'm young, free and single now.'

CHAPTER 13

BO ROMANCE RUMOURS

Bo Bruce might not have won *The Voice* but viewers and the press in particular were convinced she had won the heart of Danny. It was true that the pair had grown close and shared a chemistry on screen and off, but it was driven by a love of music, by Danny caring for her from a career perspective and by empathising with her personal heartache because of her mother's cancer. 'I knew a bit of what she was going through,' says Danny, 'and what she had to do to get out and go on stage every week was very special.'

Bo had also had to cope with a drink and drugs addiction that needed a spell in rehab, so there was no doubt that Danny felt protective of her after all she had been through. He identified too with the emotion she put into her singing. He knew better than anyone that her doe-eyed sadness was no act.

The rumours of a romance reached a new level when Danny's girlfriend Irma did not attend the final of *The Voice*, during which viewers saw him shed tears over Bo in a video tribute. Danny and Bo also sang an emotional duet, 'Read All About It', with their faces nearly touching in a lingering look and Danny resting his hand on her hip. At one point they looked as though they were about to kiss. Even host Holly Willoughby commented on it. 'That was hot, oh my goodness me!' she squealed. 'Here you are, gazing in each other's eyes ... There's that look again!'

'I'm over the moon to have Bo as my finalist,' Danny said. 'She's everything, absolutely everything. There's a lot on Bo's plate with her mother, who's incredibly sick. For her to give the performances she does ... I take my hat off to her. She's my inspiration.'

Bo, too, paid tribute to her mentor for his support on and off camera. 'This experience wouldn't have been the same if I hadn't had Danny,' she said. 'From the word go, he had confidence in me. I get on very well with Danny, we have a lot in common.'

The pair then later posted a Twitter picture of themselves drinking wine backstage, which fed the rumour mill further. One fan tweeted, 'Oh my god. Bo and Danny on *The Voice*, there is definitely something going on there. Talk about sexual tension.'

Danny and Bo also both tweeted that they had attended Coldplay's gig together, with Bo calling it 'possibly the best night of my life'.

Danny took to Twitter again in an attempt to dispel the gossip, saying that it was unfair taking the attention away from the show's actual winner. 'All these silly stories in the press, focus should be on Leanne and the brilliant job she's done,' he said. 'Well done Team Tom, what a legend.'

At this stage Danny's split from Irma had not been confirmed. Throughout the series he had always described himself as a 'one woman man' and when asked about interest from other girls he replied, 'Have you seen my girlfriend?' But days after the final the breakdown of his relationship was confirmed and it was then that Bo was suddenly cast as 'the other woman' who might have been a factor in the break-up.

'I didn't deny or confirm the speculation,' Danny told the *Daily Mail* in August 2013 while looking back on the series. 'I found it funny. By not saying anything, it created its own buzz. I thought I'd use it, and help Bo get publicity.'

Danny had involved his band-mates throughout his time on *The Voice*, and this time it was no different. 'When there was all the speculation about Danny and Bo, he told us, "This is getting out of hand,"' Mark told the *Daily Mail*. 'But I said we could use all the attention to help her. Me and Glen would go out the back of the studio and have a cigarette with her. We could easily have been photographed with her, and people could have said the same thing about either of us – that we were in a relationship with her.'

The true story, said Danny, was that he and Bo were close, but that was because he was still working with her and had co-written her single 'Alive'. But the fact that they were often pictured out together only fuelled the speculation. 'It was always promotional stuff for the show,' Danny told *The Times* in March 2013. 'It got a bit silly but ... it was always about the music for me.'

At the height of that silliness Danny asked Mark for advice on how to handle the attention. 'I had paparazzi hiding behind bushes,' Danny told *The Times*. 'It was ridiculous. I mean, what kind of shot are you going to get from behind a bush? He [Mark] said, "Don't do anything. Don't fan the flames." He pointed out that it had created the kind of publicity money can't buy, so I accepted that in the end and it wasn't particularly damaging and it got Bo's name everywhere so ...'

As far as Danny was concerned, the hassle was worth it if it meant Bo getting the chance to make it as an artist in her own right. 'It's the right voice with the right look so ... it's all going well for her and I am happy about that,' he said. 'In all honesty, I will do anything to get people to listen to music, proper music. Bands are in danger of losing an audience. *The Voice* encourages singing and songwriting and that's why it's great. It's not a talent show in the way *X Factor* is.'

The prying eyes of the press and paparazzi would not stop Danny from stepping out with Bo as he knew he had nothing to hide. At the end of June they hit the town in London at private members club and celeb hangout the

Groucho Club, sharing a smoke just inside the club's front doors after attending the *Britain Creates* gala at the Old Selfridges Hotel, where Bo had enjoyed an animated conversation with Princess Beatrice.

Afterwards, in an interview with Capital breakfast duo Lisa Snowdon and Dave Berry, Danny again denied they were seeing each other. 'There's nothing, nothing going on,' he told them and laughed when they asked if he had 'dipped his pen in the company ink'. 'No, no, not at all,' he said. 'This story came out of nowhere. We were on TV, we had this moment where we were face to face – part of the BBC choreography is that you listen to the choreographer and do what they're saying. It was one of those moments on TV where everybody went, "Oh, saucy – there's something going on there." Not at all, no.'

For months Danny was forced to keep denying constant rumours in the press that his break-up with Irma had anything to do with Bo. 'That was hurtful to me, hurtful to my ex and hurtful to everyone involved,' he told the *Irish Mail on Sunday*.

But fame comes at a price and Danny's raised profile thanks to *The Voice* saw his personal life scrutinised to levels he could never have imagined. He was shocked when he witnessed some of the levels of intrusion. 'My sister, who has a small business, has a Facebook page,' he told the *Irish Times*. 'She told me that she received a message from a certain media outlet saying that they would happily give her space if she wanted to talk about

"Danny's side of the love split story". But what really got to her, and me, was the offer of money to her if she talked, and also the knowledge they had about her business – the paper said they would promote it in their pages if she talked to them.'

'I've been put through the ringer,' he confided to the *Irish Independent*. 'It is one of the hardest things I have ever done in my life. But the split happened about a month before the show started.'

'It's scary now as that has been on the chopping block a bit,' Danny told the *Sun* about living with his private life spilled over the newspapers. 'It's been hard. I'd escape from the pain of the break-up by going into the studio. Every problem I have, I always go into the studio as I feel safe in a padded room. I could deal with it all fine but it was all those crazy rumours of who I was dating. There was also a big-time difference between me breaking up and all the other stuff.'

But as with every emotional twist and turn in his life, Danny drew inspiration from it and the break-up supplied him with the song 'Six Degrees of Separation'. Danny told the *Irish Mail on Sunday* he had felt compelled to write it. 'It wasn't a choice, it just happened. I don't sit down with the decision to just write, I just had to get it out. It is an on-going thing and it still evolves. The song is the way I felt at that time. It's probably a song I'll write another verse for in a year's time because it is still pretty fresh.

'Songs are emotional and you write about what you

feel and are attached to. And obviously it is a testament to how much she meant to me that it found its way out into art. And that's the way it is. You never think of the consequences when you are being creative, you just deal with them after. I am at the sixth stage right now. You have to listen to the song to know what that is. The sixth is when you admit you may have fucked up a little.'

Danny also admitted that living his private life in public had been a huge learning process for him. 'This is the band's first time of dealing with the spotlight. I've been asked why I let the rumours go on for so long. But there's no handbooks on how to deal with this, plus I was grieving. My relationship had ended.'

'Danny is my best mate, like a brother, and I know Irma really well,' Mark told the *Irish Daily Mail*. 'It was a lovely break-up. They were such adults. I have never seen such a break-up where two people can be friends. Then suddenly people thought he was with Bo, an artist that I was recording with. They had no interest in taking a picture of me when I was in the studio with her or outside smoking a cigarette with her – they wanted him. And that's the bullet that we dodged and Danny is constantly taking.'

Danny told the *Irish Mirror* in August 2012 that the rumours around Bo hurt because he was already being put through the ringer with his split from Irma. 'Nobody ever heard it from me,' he said. 'But what was really interesting was over the course of a few weeks after *The Voice* they were so obsessed with that story that Leanne didn't get a look in, Jessie didn't get a look in with Vince but Bo was in the press for literally two months straight. So we were thinking, "I can stop this right now and say there's nothing going on," but we thought, "Why not leave it?" She's been in the press now for two months. And I feel now we have bridged the gap between *The Voice* and her album and single and kept her in the marketplace.

'Myself and Mark wrote a song for Bo, it's fucking amazing. I think she could be the next Dido. I believe in her voice – her voice is incredible and that is why she got where she is.'

Again Mark was quick to back his buddy over the rumours. 'What people don't know is I am backstage with these people talking about writing songs and so on,' he told the *Irish Mirror*. 'No one ever takes a picture of me and Bo hugging – it's not interesting because I am married. But they latch on to a break-up he had and put two and two together. I thought it was a bad thing for her career and then I thought, "If we want to get her name out there we should say nothing, ride the wave." Now people know this girl and we could never have afforded to pay for the press and publicity she got.

'Bo's a very loveable girl – if you met Bo Bruce in a room she is really friendly, she is a huggy type of girl. His problem was he never denied it but that was the only issue. He never went public and said, "I'm not." But that was our call too – we thought we could help an artist and I think we have.'

Danny, who assured reporters that he was in fact 'very single', opened up more to the *Irish Daily Mail*, telling them that the rumours were simply hurtful gossip, which he had decided to ignore. 'It was really upsetting at the time,' he said. 'I was used to seeing fans outside my flat only this time they were replaced by men in long coats and lenses snapping away.

'But I was still coming to terms with the break-up and then I had this shit thrown at me and it was all rubbish. People assumed that because I was passionate about Bo that we were together. The truth is that I am working with her and we decided to let the story run to keep her name in the papers so that she was still in the public sphere when she releases a single. We decided to play them at their own game.'

As time progressed, Danny grew tired of being hit by the same old questions over Bo Bruce. 'I don't have much to say about Bo,' he said. 'Everybody wants to fan the flames, so I'm happy to let them churn out their stuff. People want me to respond, but I'm not going to.'

Bo, meanwhile, was facing similar questions, even though it was barely a month since she had buried her mother, who had lost her six-month battle with pancreatic cancer. Danny, knowing what it is like to experience the loss of a parent, helped her channel that 'explosion' of emotions into her songwriting. As well as

The Script, she would write with Gary Lightbody and Snow Patrol as well as Athlete.

'It's funny, I went into the show with this whole will.i.am thing and I still love him,' Bo told the *Daily Mirror* in August 2012. 'But in the blind audition with Danny, I thought, "You and I could be mates." That's always been important to me in who I work with. I was going through a lot and it was something Danny had been through. There was the intensity in that and we were really good mates. It's a confusing thing – people can't just be mates, but I've always had boy mates.'

'If you're going to put yourself in the limelight, then you have to expect it,' says Danny. 'But my life is genuinely an open book. People don't need to read about it in the press. It's all in my songs.'

'Danny and I became good friends when he was mentoring me on the show, but there really was nothing romantic to it,' Bo told the *Sun*. 'Musically, he understood me 100 per cent and people confused that for something more intimate. Plus, he had a gorgeous Amazonian girlfriend at the time. What were people thinking?!

'We were incredibly close and he's a hot guy. It was a mad time and meeting someone under those circumstances is difficult. I was very vulnerable and I regret a lot of things that happened. There was such an obsession with whether or not we were together and that put wild amounts of pressure on us.

'In the end a decision was made for him to not be

around me. The process of writing my album *Before I Sleep* began when I was supposed to go with Danny to a Coldplay concert. It was meant to be an end of *The Voice* present – for him and me. But he was told he was not allowed to, because he couldn't be seen with me in public. So I ended up not going with him but someone took pity on me and invited me to Coldplay's box, with Coldplay's agent, who then wanted to sign me. So although I said I have regrets about what happened, it led to so many other things.'

'It was an incredible whirlwind, that show,' she told *New!* magazine. 'There was so much rumour and pressure on us, it was mad. I was going through a lot at that time and I was possibly looking to him for more help than he would be able to give under the circumstances with what the press were saying to us.'

She said 'Alive', the song she co-wrote with Danny, 'deals with regret and who the last person would be that you thought of at night or at the end of your life.' She'd wanted Danny to be in the video for the song but his timetable didn't allow it.

Ahead of a UK tour, Bo performed a number of tracks to a select audience. 'I did ask Danny to come along,' she told the *Daily Mail*. 'I was a bit disappointed he wasn't there.

'I've never discussed in public whether he and I were ever an item and I never will. Anything I've ever said addressed our friendship but it was misinterpreted as being about a so-called relationship. It was a crazy time;

we were both flung into the limelight and I was competing in *The Voice* and Mum was dying, and that's a lot of pressure for any fledgling relationship to bear.'

CHAPTER 14

THREE'S
A CHARM

On 23 July 2012 Epic Records announced in New York that The Script were to release their third album – #3 – on 9 October. On the same day they were to kick off an 18-date headline tour of major cities in North America, starting at Radio City Music Hall in New York.

'We have bared all on the new album and really bled on the page,' Danny told the *Evening Express*. 'Emotionally we have reached another level and I am so proud to release a record where our hearts are on our sleeves. However, we made sure we produced big banging anthems that you can sing and dance to. The mantra for this album was the head, heart and feet. We wanted to produce something you could think about, but dance to at the same time.'

The first single from the new album was the collaboration with will.i.am from *The Voice*, 'Hall of Fame', released on 21 August in the US and 2 September in the UK. Mark confessed that all along the plan had been to use Danny's links to will.i.am to boost their global profile, especially in America. 'He has been so big over there for years so hopefully it will help us a bit and in places like France and Germany where we're not that big either,' he said.

But the plan almost backfired – the song was so good that will.i.am wanted it for himself. 'He heard it and I think he loved the song,' Danny told Capital FM's *Breakfast Show*. 'He was like, "I need this for my album – please can I have this for my album?"'

Danny told listeners that getting the chance to work with Will had been like a dream come true. 'I grew up listening to all of his stuff – you know, "Request Line" back in the old days when Fergie wasn't in the band. So to finally have this come full circle and to actually be working with a hero of mine as well, it was really strange,' he said.

'I told him he couldn't have it, so he agreed to guest on it instead. Then, when we arranged a session, he flaked out because he had been invited to dinner with Bill Clinton!' Danny joked that it had taken several months to finally get Will to record his part.

Mark took up the story in an interview with Dublin radio station FM104's *Strawberry Alarm Clock*. 'Will.i.am wanted to record the song for his own album but Danny said no because we wrote it together. I was backstage at *The Voice* and he asked me. I said, "Cool – as long as we're on the song with you." He wasn't really into that at the time.

'One night Danny got him in a headlock and put him in a cab and we recorded a song in 30 minutes. I ran out of that place with a hard drive with his vocals on it in my bag like I had just robbed a bank! He was happy enough with it – he actually added a really cool part.'

'We taped his lines in a hotel room,' Danny added. 'It must have been strange for him to be caught in a headlock in his own hotel by two Irish blokes.

'As we left the room, we were thanking Will and all his crew were there – we were doing the big high-fives and hip-hop hugs. We walked outside the door and, as soon as we did, we silently punched the air – a total smash and grab. We had to be as a cool as shit in the room with all the boys, but outside we really let it go.'

Danny told the *Daily Star* the story behind the song. 'I hate the idea of getting famous just for being famous. People say: "How can you say that when you did *The Voice*?" but I did the show to represent bands. Our message is, don't be famous for fame's sake. Be a teacher, a politician, whatever, but get on your soapbox and say something – don't expect to get it on a plate. My lyrics come from deep-rooted issues. I'm sure there's some computer program that could be written to analyse it because I get all the dark stuff out in The Script.'

The band would get a welcome boost with the aptly

titled anthem featuring repeatedly in TV coverage of the Olympic Games in London. But at the start of August, more than a month before #3 was due to be released in the UK and Ireland, the band faced a new problem: their new album was being shared on the internet.

'It's already leaked,' Danny told the *Irish Independent*. 'I've seen it in snippets. We're living in a day and age where some people who download, don't buy music so you just build it into your business model. For instance, we go to places like Johannesburg and Cape Town, where we don't have massive record sales but we can sell out a 16,000-seater stadium, and they knew the words to all our songs. Well, they must be getting them from somewhere.'

One track on the new album, 'If You Could See Me Now', was powerful stuff emotionally. It deals with the devastating blow of losing a parent and initially Mark could hardly bear to listen to it, let alone play it in public.

'I need a minute with that song,' Mark admitted to the *Irish Mail on Sunday*. 'It's a page from my diary. I produced and wrote it but I have to walk away from it. It is just a weird one. It is a touchy subject for me – I lost both my parents quite young and it was a real dark point in my life. It is something I have never talked about until now. I don't know if we will ever find the right moment to play that live at all. I can't even picture playing it live because it is so personal.'

Danny, who has shared Mark's pain, was close to tears on the subject. He knows that although he lost his dad Shay, at least his father had seen some measure of his success and his mum has been able to watch her son soar to stardom.

'Mark's mum and dad have never seen him cry, have never seen the success or got to hear him put himself out there emotionally,' he told the *Irish Mail on Sunday*. 'To hear how he can so eloquently say what I couldn't say was really great for me. To know everything he went through to put in his verse and what I went through for mine is a coming-of-age thing for both of us. It was an Everest moment for us. And we both held each other's hands and just jumped off.

'I'm bulletproof with any of the other stuff. If it is received well or not, it is no skin off my nose because I have this song. It means the world to me and Mark and that's all that matters.'

'That song is all about two grown men sitting down and dealing with things,' he explained to the *Daily Mail*. 'With that song, Mark and I left the realm of songwriters and began to bare our souls. It's not a look-at-me song. It's us wondering what our parents would think of us now. They'd probably tell me I drink and smoke too much, but I think they'd also be proud.'

Mark added to the *Sun*: 'We're quite happy lads in real life but we just vent everything in our music. We wear our hearts on our sleeves and put everything into our music. "If You Could See Me Now" is the first time we've rinsed ourselves that deeply. There's been a lot bottled up and we felt there was a hole in the album and we weren't being honest enough until this song.

'We really hit the whiskies one night, that was the catalyst. We were very emotional and wrote a song about this – Danny one end of the room, me at another. It was a tough one to write and I didn't want anyone to listen to it at first, if I'm honest. But that's what we're in music for – that honest emotion. I'm so proud of that song.'

'It was an incredibly hard song to write,' Danny added to *The Independent*. 'As soon as I started writing the lyrics, I started crying. We're men, we're 30 years old, and there's not a lot of people out there that would be open enough to say it in the same way as The Script. That song was more important for Mark than it was for me because I'm very open about my emotions, but he's not at all, so to hear him sum up in one verse what I've been waiting for him to say to me was an incredible moment. That really is the power of music.'

'And when we were recording that we were looking at each other across the studio as if to say, "Are you OK with this?" ' Danny told the Press Association. 'But it turns out it's one of the best things we've done. I'll remember that night for the rest of my life. Emotionally, we achieved exactly what we got in to music for, what we're all still in it for. Not the number one singles or the fame, but to capture an emotion in three and a half minutes that we know will mean an awful lot to other people.

'I'm biased, I know, but I think Mark's second verse on that song is one of the best ever. Mark's lyrics are so eloquent, and articulate. He's never talked about it before, not because he didn't want to, but because he couldn't. He's clearly thought about his parents to the point where it now rhymes and makes so much sense that it'll have people in tears, I'm sure of it.

'As a band, writing that song was the bravest thing we've ever done. It's us imagining what our parents would say were they still here. We like to think they would be proud of us and our achievements, but they'd probably be telling us off for drinking and smoking and swearing too much. And you know what? They'd be right.'

The band held an exclusive listening launch party for *#3* in Dublin's Windmill Lane Studios for select members of the media. At the event Danny told the *Irish Mail on Sunday* that fans of The Script had gone to incredible lengths to try and get close to their heroes – one had even forged a backstage pass at a London gig the year before.

'She printed up her own security jacket and got a press pass printed up,' he revealed. 'She got them laminated and everything and was really convincing. She was standing on the stage watching but her mistake was she jumped into a lift with us, and the only people allowed in were the band and our security guard. I wasn't that mad, to be honest. I was fairly impressed because she did an amazing job.

'There's one [fan] who direct messages us every three hours, day and night. She is talking to us like she is a best friend – "I miss you" and so on.'

Danny also revealed more about his love of photography, and his directing a video for the proposed single 'Broken Arrow'. 'I've been majorly into photography for the past few years,' he revealed. 'On St Patrick's Day myself and another photographer shot 24 hours in Dublin. We got to some really cool places. I got up on top of Liberty Hall as well as Bono's penthouse in the Clarence and then the window in the balcony in the Olympia. It's something I'm really passionate about.'

They had initially set out to be a faceless band, but now, thanks to Danny's profile on *The Voice*, Danny was getting mobbed for photos and autographs. 'Of course, Glen and I didn't mind he was getting all the attention,' says Mark. 'It's good for the band as a whole.'

But The Script still try to keep their feet on the ground, and that includes making time for fans for photos and autographs when they can. Danny and Mark have even been known to entertain young fans with magic tricks when they bump into them in hotels or suchlike.

'We'll never get big-headed,' Mark told the *Sun*. 'I won't even put our awards and discs up at home. When I moved into my house I didn't know what to do with them. I thought it was showing off. We do get recognised now. I say "we" but I mean Danny. I can escape without a fuss, which is great. I look like Ming The Merciless next to him, so they leave me alone.'

'It's fine having people come up to you,' Danny added, 'but there are times when you could do without it. Like, I was getting my passport photos done and didn't want to be there, I was tired, and suddenly this guy next to me was talking into his phone. Only he didn't realise he was shouting and I could hear: "OH, IT'S DANNY FROM THE SCRIPT! YOU KNOW, DANNY FROM THE VOICE!" He was screaming like that. So I joined in: "I DON'T KNOW YOUR BLEEDING NAME BUT I'M GOING TO SHOUT RIGHT BACK AT YOU!"

'He was shouting: "JESUS CHRIST, DANNY FROM THE SCRIPT IS SO TALL!" So I was shouting back: "JESUS CHRIST, YOU'RE SMALL!" But it was all a bit of fun and comes with the realisation of a dream for us.'

Danny reiterated once more, need it be said, that for him it's all about pleasing his fans and selling records without fearing what the critics would think. 'Someone told us that if you had acclaim and great reviews you wouldn't have the sales,' he said. 'So we're happy with the sales, thank you very much.

'Elton John said something nice: that there's not many bands that write, produce and perform their music like The Script. He said you can tell we've quality-controlled everything from the lyrics, the melodies, the experience. That's all so important.'

Like any good Irishman, Danny is partial to a pint of Guinness and the album opener 'Good Ol' Days' reflects the band's philosophy of enjoying music but having fun too. 'For ages, a Script song would be about singing your heart out in the car but you couldn't dance to a song. But there's a few songs on this album that you can put on in a bar now. "Good Ol' Days" was inspired by our mates in Dublin. We go down the pub with them when we are home and we see what they say we should do next.'

Mark revealed that while Danny's stint on *The Voice* had been a strategic move agreed by all three band members, it hadn't been all plain sailing as they battled to find time to make the new album. 'I was spending all day in the studio, and Danny would arrive at 7pm,' Mark says. 'I needed his undivided attention, but he would be tired. We had some screaming rows, but it was never personal. It was always about the music.'

'It was quite an exciting time for us as a band with him on the television and us recording the album at the same time,' he told the *Daily Mirror*. 'We have always written and produced everything at the same time since we were 14, then all of a sudden he's on the television and I am in the studio trying to make sense of an album. He had to work overtime and come in after he was finished in the BBC and work for 12 hours on an album.'

When it came to promoting the new album, Danny was in his element with his charm and wise-cracking. 'I like talking,' he told the Press Association, 'and my favourite subject is us, the band. We're on a promo marathon at the moment, or Promogeddon as we like to call it.

'We set off at the start of the year saying it would be brilliant if I could do *The Voice* AND have an album done in the background. We didn't think it would be possible, but that was the aim. Anyway, Mark and Glen were working during the day when I was filming, and I'd join them in the recording studio afterwards.

'Sometimes I'd be filming from 9am until 9pm, but I'd go straight to meet them and we'd work 'til 2 or 3am. It was really hard, but we're in this game to get things done and work hard. Bring it on, we say. Not many bands would even contemplate doing what we did, but we ended up delivering the record two months early, which is unheard of. We were militant in our attack.'

Initially Danny had been worried that sitting in a TV studio all day might stifle his creativity. As it turned out, coaching the contestants, picking out songs for them, writing harmonies and working alongside three other professional singers had had quite the opposite effect.

'I used to hear stories about the Rolling Stones coming off stage somewhere and going straight to the studio, and I could never get my head around it, but it's because their energy was high and the adrenaline kept them going,' he said, perhaps underestimating what other chemicals might have been keeping the Stones going into the wee hours.

'It was a bit like that with *The Voice*, I suppose. It's all music and I was buzzing all day. People like me and will.i.am, you can't stop us. We have music everywhere, and will make music anywhere. Even in my trailer at *The Voice* I had a little recording studio. I can't be anywhere without one.'

The proof of that was 'Hall of Fame', the lead single from #3. One of the most-played songs on the radio in the UK, the US, large parts of Europe, Australia and New Zealand, it was ready to be crowned the most successful song The Script have had. As it hit No 1 in the UK and Ireland, climbed to No 25 in the Billboard Hot

100 and charted across Europe and Australasia, The Script played three gigs in four days in Glasgow, Manchester and London to keep them match-fit for their assault on the US.

As the band had hoped, *The Voice* had changed everything, although not always in the way they had hoped. 'It used to be girls hanging around outside my house, but now it's guys in trench coats – the paparazzi,' Danny told the *Irish Times* as they launched the album in Dublin. 'That's the big change in doing a big prime-time TV show. Sure, I got recognised before, but now it's just insane. The other night in London we all went out for drinks together – myself, Mark and Glen. The story the next day in the papers was "Danny goes drinking with his two bodyguards."'

Mark, however, felt a sense of satisfaction about their move to give Danny the time off from the band to do the show. 'People knew who The Script were but we wanted a "face" for the band, and Danny being on TV gave us that,' he told the *Irish Times*. 'When he went on the first episode it was all "Who is that guy?" but now everyone knows him and, by extension, everyone knows The Script. I know there will be people saying real musicians shouldn't be doing TV judging competitions but I've been around the music industry almost 20 years now and with the state the business is in now, if you don't take these opportunities to promote your band you will starve to death.

'We were all for Danny doing the show. I've done all

the years of making tea for a living, trying to get a bit of session work here and there. Over in the US, I was living in places infested with cockroaches and hearing gunshots down the road. Myself and Danny were over in the States for years after the boy band didn't take off and it was hard. We felt like giving up more than once but then we'd get a chance to remix a Justin Timberlake track or something and we'd keep on hanging on in there. I know exactly what Danny doing *The Voice* has done for this band's profile.'

'To give you an example,' added Danny, 'when we arrived back into Dublin airport we were all starving and all we wanted was Burger King. Now, I know we can use the airport lounges and all of that but we were determined to go to Burger King. We knew what it would mean – people asking for autographs and stopping to talk about a particular song and what it means to them – and that did happen but that's fine. You won't hear us complaining about fame after what we've been through on the way up.

'I remember the editor of [a certain well known music magazine] who had slated us in print coming over to me after a gig and looking for autographs for all of his family – that made me laugh.'

The Script felt they were getting better with age and that #3 was their most accomplished album to date. As usual, however, all their innermost secrets and emotions were laid bare – love and loss, life and death, break-ups and romance, and above all else the eternal underlying theme of hope.

'Trying to get it played on the radio is the number one priority not just for us but for any band,' Danny told the *Daily Mirror*. 'You hope those three singles will entice people to come in to listen to the rest of your art. For us it is always about being personal, it is the only way to get people emotionally involved in your music. It's about honesty, putting your heart out there. I feel personally it is a really good time for the band because we are just getting it right now.'

Danny admitted to the *Scottish Sun* that there was another secret to getting their creative juices flowing – single malt whisky. 'Mark is massively into his Scotch,' he said. 'He loves a bit of Laphroaig, Talisker, the Isle of Islay, all that. We write our best stuff when we're on the whisky. A lovely bit of single malt gets you down to this place where you're emotional but you're secure and confident in that emotion. A gin and tonic takes it too far and you end up depressed. So we get on the malts and we go to these places – and say the things we want to tell the world.

'A lot of people in music want to be aggressive and say they are too cool for school – and it's all this, "I'm in the club, rub a dub, getting some love, wearing black gloves,"' he explained. 'The emotion that we put in our songs – people are dying for it. They've heard enough shit on the radio nowadays, so when an act like Ed Sheeran or Adele comes along, it just stands out against everything else. They are incredibly gifted people and there's more out there.

'But the reason why those two, for example, seem so amazing is because of the backdrop of modern-day music. There are great lyrics and melodies out there, but you won't get them as there's so much rubbish. If you give them pop music that is throwaway, then they'll throw you away. That's a very important lesson to learn: you can give them one or two dance club songs but unless you're giving something substantial then you're in real trouble. Music is a one-sided conversation and unless you like deeply what that person is saying, you're going to fucking forget about it.'

Juggling *The Voice* and The Script's new album had been a huge workload but Danny had faced the challenge head-on. 'We had maybe two ideas which were guitar riffs heading into the show,' he told the *Scottish Sun*. 'That was the sticking point, whether we were going to be able to write this album and do the show at the same time. We said, if we really worked at it, we could. Mark was in the studio during the day, I was there at night. We both still produced the record, there was no extra help – we were up against it but anyone who knows this band, knows we fucking crave hard work.'

With both their previous albums having topped the UK charts and made a serious dent in the US, the boys had felt they could handle things better the third time around.

'On the first album, you're flying around the world like a deer in the headlights,' Danny told the same newspaper. 'But, on the second one, you're seeing the same people and you realise it's a world that you can get to grips with.

So on this one, we're comfortable in our skin. Before the three of us would do interviews together, but now they don't mind me doing it alone or one of the others does it.

'It's taken time to get here, but the dynamics of how we work are still as fucked up as they ever were. Everybody knows, you just get me and the band whatever way we are on a particular day. We've always left cool behind – you can't be fucking cool singing about emotional stuff. And you can't tell The Script what to do. We do what we want.'

Indeed Danny was not averse to taking revenge on James Corden when the *Sun* brought up his infamous cruel jibe at the Brits. 'I haven't bumped into him – I'd be more likely to bump off him,' he joked. 'There was a good 15 minutes when I thought I was going to throw a bun at his head. But karma intervened and he fucked the whole thing up by cutting Adele's speech short.'

As an added publicity stunt while they were back home in Dublin, the guys joined some student buskers in the popular Temple Bar area for a couple of songs. As many as 300 fans enjoyed the impromptu 'flash' gig outside the Button Factory, announced just an hour earlier on their Twitter account.

In September Danny gave one of his raunchiest ever interviews to the *Sunday Mirror* as part of their 'Five minutes with a sex god' feature. First they asked if he had received more female attention as a by-product of starring on *The Voice*. 'Definitely,' agreed Danny. 'I think it's just the telly thing. You can look like a twat and people still ask for your phone number. I don't know if it's a compliment, but people come up to me in the street and say, "Holy shit, you're tall." Everyone seems to like my hair too.'

After saying that he found it 'just weird' to be labelled a sex god, Danny went on to tell them what he finds sexiest in a woman. 'I do love a girl who can make me laugh,' he admitted. 'When you're older, you'll be grey and ugly, so when all that superficial shit has gone, at least you can have a giggle on the couch.'

He then admitted he uses his accent to charm women – 'When you're in America it's like having a superpower' – and revealed his best chat-up line. 'The one we pull out all the time is, "Me and my friend were having a bet about your nationality and I think I won. What is it?" Then they go, "Oh right, who bet on what?" and you tell them. That works but you can say anything just to get in the door, even if it's "Do you like cucumbers?"'

He also said he prefers women to have a nice bum rather than boobs and, modest as ever, told the paper that he'd give himself 10 out of 10 in the bedroom. 'I love giving massages,' was his answer to how he gets in the mood for love. 'I love to give pleasure. You have to look after your woman.'

Refreshingly, he said that when in a relationship he is totally committed, but added cheekily that when single he can't be held responsible. 'There is a lot of security in a relationship,' he said. 'But when you're single you never know what will happen and there's a massive amount of freedom. I was a serial monogamist, but now the cord has been cut and I'm like a helium balloon.'

And when you are a good-looking frontman for a hugely popular rock band, there is no shortage of propositions from adoring fans. 'I get loads,' he confessed. 'I've been invited back by a whole house of sorority girls in America because they were having some kind of ping-pong party or something. Unfortunately we were on tour and everywhere we went we had to be on the bus by 2am so we couldn't do much.'

Had he ever been caught in the act of sex? 'Yeah! And purposely. I'm a naughty man, me.'

The newspaper also asked him if he were to have a threesome with two celebrity women, who would they be? 'Oh my God, I can't answer that,' he gasped, before adding: 'Jessie J and Ellie Goulding. No, I'm joking. Jessie is going to tweet the hell out of me for saying that. Jessie is gorgeous and she knows it. She's just a stunning person and really beautiful. I used to tell her all the time on *The Voice*. I'd just look over and go, "You're gorgeous, you are!"'

On the subject of music, Danny knew The Script could never win when it came to the critics. 'People have accused us of selling out and being too pop,' he told *Daily Star Sunday*. 'But what they call selling out, I call common sense. The radio is the porthole to the world for an artist. You can either play to 30 people in a wanky bar or learn how to write classic pop songs. It's not rocket science. It doesn't mean you have to lose your credibility as an artist.

'The mantra when we set out was that we wanted to make everyone in the world hear a Script song at least once. And it seems like we're doing a pretty good job. But no, it's just about trying to make the music we want to make and pouring our heart and soul into that.'

And heading to No 1 with 'Hall of Fame' had left Jessie J talking about following suit. 'Jessie was saying that lyrically on her next album she wants to articulate the break-up she went through, so I was like: "Come to me. No one can write love songs like me!" I would love to write with her – her voice is incredible. She has the whole world in her hands.'

Danny says that he and Mark would often have ferocious rows – sometimes so bad that he had thought The Script were on the verge of splitting up. 'It's got close to being serious loads of times,' Danny told the *Daily Star*. 'If anyone from the label witnesses us fighting, they're in agony, because at those moments we fucking hate each other. But 10 minutes later, it's all forgotten. I love Mark, but you wouldn't think that if you saw us after a bad gig. It's never come to blows, but we have proper screaming rows over breakfast. It's always to better the band.'

The Script embarked on an extensive promo tour to promote #3. In Singapore, Danny enthused to the *Straits Times* about how many opportunities *The Voice* UK had opened up for the band. 'Without that show, we wouldn't have met Will, wouldn't have recorded "Hall of Fame" and wouldn't have our first number one single. Nothing fazes him. He's an engineer, he's tweeting, producing, arranging, doing the vocals all at the same time. He's capable and a Zen guy.

'Before this, we used to hide our hip hop roots in little bits of the melody and verses, because we didn't think people would accept it. Obviously we're white and we're from Ireland – it'd be weird to go: "Here's a hip hop group from Ireland." So we got people into our music little by little.'

Whisky might have helped to get the creative juices flowing for #3, but vodka shots are the order of the day before going on stage. 'It affects us in the good way,' Danny told the *Daily Mirror*. 'We don't go too mad – we need something to loosen us up a little bit. Usually what we do is exactly 30 minutes before stage we do a shot of vodka with cranberry. It's a two-fingered shot. It's doubled in size lately. But there definitely would have been many times when we've had a good bit more than that. And of course, we're on stage getting warm and people want to give us lots of beer. It's very hot on stage, it's thirsty work.'

Despite the band's hectic schedule, Danny still remained true to his word to make time to help his proteges from *The Voice*. 'We've had both Bo [Bruce] and Max [Milner] in the recording studio with us,' he told *Daily Star Sunday*. 'We wrote a song for Bo, which sounds amazing. I think it should be her first single and I honestly think she's going to become a huge star. I'm enjoying being Danny from The Script again rather than Danny from *The Voice*.

'It's nice having the day job back,' he quipped. 'After *The Voice* I was just relieved I didn't come over too much like the knobhead we all know I am.'

After a stellar sell-out show in London, Mark told the *Irish Daily Mail*: 'Danny loves being a lead singer. The perfect football team is when the keeper loves being a keeper, a defender loves to be a defender and a manager loves to manage. I'm not interested in being a lead vocalist and I never have been, [though] I quite enjoy backing vocals, and I quite enjoy backing him up.

'Danny is able to handle all the limelight and is polite to photographers, whereas I'll probably tell them to fuck off. You don't want me on *The Voice* because I'll tell someone exactly what I think. I'd turn it into *The Mouth* and just offend people. I'm not a lead man in that way.

'How do I feel about Danny on *The Voice*? To be honest I am happy for him one week and I am embarrassed the next. While he is there dancing on his chair I'm at home throwing popcorn at the television. But he is my mate and that's the way it is. I mightn't like what he says on the TV but then I wouldn't do it and he is there for all three of us. And there are times in the studio when I embarrass him. That's the way it goes. That's what any relationship is like.'

'I felt sorry for Danny,' Glen added. 'He did us proud [on *The Voice*]. You are always worried for him in case he says the wrong thing and it is a big spotlight for anyone. But if you asked anyone before *The Voice* if they knew who The Script was, they would have looked at you with a blank expression. If you played them "Breakeven" they would know the song but they wouldn't have known the group.

'We felt that if he did the show we would finally be able to put a face with the band. And he paid a price for that. I do feel sorry for Danny because he had to sacrifice his anonymity. I went out with him in London and we pulled up to [private club] Soho House and 14 guys appeared out of nowhere with a camera. It was like they jumped out of a dustbin. I got out the other side of the car and they didn't bat an eyelid at me. The minute that he got out he was hounded. It was unreal. I saw the darker side of the business and how negative it can be and I never want to be involved in that.'

Danny was again at pains to stress it had all been part of their plan to build up to this point. They had always set out to work from the bottom up and it had never been about him or a specific image for the band.

'It was very much our choice,' he told *The Independent.* 'We didn't have ourselves on the front cover [of our albums] because we didn't want people to get the wrong idea about this band. It's very easy for a record company to package a band as extremely pop, a band that could be really easily confused with a McFly. We didn't want to be perceived in any way other than the music and creativity.'

Despite the trappings of fame, Danny is not one for *MTV Cribs*-style mansions. 'The boys have all moved, but I'm still in the shitty bedsit,' he said. 'This isn't going to be forever, so why would you say, "Oh, I've got a bit of money now, let's go live in The Hamptons?" A lot of my friends don't have money, and I would hate to lose touch with all of my friends and family. I don't have any plaques on my wall; I'm not into it at all. When you're dead and buried, that's for other people to celebrate your life. I'm living it.'

Danny also uses a cunning plan to minimise the chances of being mobbed out on his own in the big city. 'I wear fake wigs and hats whenever I go out now,' he says. 'So if you see a 6ft 4in strange-looking guy, it's probably me. I wear an Aztec hat with dog ears and sometimes sunglasses and a big puffy jacket. In the street it buys you that extra two seconds before they go "Is that…?" and then you are past.'

Disguises only work up to a point, however – even in fancy dress. 'I went to a party as Edward Scissorhands,' he said. 'Black make-up. Hair all over the place. I still had two girls chasing me down the road screaming, "I'd know that walk anywhere!"'

Danny also let the world in on a secret about his life on the road. 'I am now getting them to book me into the same room number at every hotel we stay in,' he admits. 'That way I can always get back to my bed even after a big night out. The boys keep threatening to tweet that room number just to see who turns up!'

In November it was back to the US. Their favourite haunt *The Today Show* on NBC was a staple in New York, but they would also be playing the city's Radio City

Music Hall – the largest indoor theatre in the world at 6,000 capacity and dubbed 'the showplace of the nation' – and an after-show party, where Liam Neeson was among the guests. They then jetted to Los Angeles for *The Ellen DeGeneres Show*, where will.i.am gave everyone a scare.

'When we performed "Hall of Fame" together on the *Ellen* show, Will got there at the last second, said Mark. 'The curtain was about to go up and we were like: "Please, please turn up." Then he did. It was live.'

The response The Script get from their fans at their gigs never fails to move the band. Danny told the *Sunday Telegraph*'s *Seven* magazine that even in the US he never fears reaching out his microphone to the crowd to sing back to him. 'No, because as a performer it is up to you to sense whether they will respond or not, so there are some nights I hold back,' he said. 'We have these in-ear monitors on stage which block out the sound of the crowd so we can hear ourselves sing, and the first time it happened I popped them out and was blown away. A giant choir of 60,000 people singing my own song back to me. It was overwhelming. I almost choked.

'The adrenaline does mean that three hours after a gig we're not going to sleep,' he added. 'We're in a bubble. When we finish the show we are transported out really quick to an after-show party where we meet record company people, then we're back on the bus doing our stretching exercises so as we don't pull muscles, and then we sleep as we drive through the night to the next town.'

Mark has always been the business brain in the band – he

negotiated all their record deals and in the early years was their manager. 'Our thinking was that no one else was going to look after our money like we would,' Danny told *Seven* magazine. 'When we first got money I wanted to go and blow it on Rolexes and cars and bollocks, but Mark wouldn't let me. He made us pay off our debts then put it in the bank. We paid ourselves a small wage and we still do.'

'Our only demand is that we are kept supplied with tea and Grey Goose vodka,' adds Mark of life on the road. 'The only other thing we have before a gig is Epsom salts for our muscles. Seriously. They keep you supple.'

'Being on the road can drive you mad,' Danny told the *Daily Mirror*, the morning before the Radio City show, sipping coffee in a New York hotel bar. 'A lot of people have likened it to being in jail. I think that's why a lot of rock stars take to drink and drugs – to take their mind off the craziness. It's a hard balance to strike because you need to be in the best physical shape you can.'

It's a sensible approach from a down-to-earth band – grounded lads who try to be the same as they always have been when they are back home in Dublin.

'Even for us, friends who were always around all the time in Dublin unfortunately put you on a pedestal,' said Danny. 'When we go to the local bar they see a different person walking in but for me I am the same, ordering the same drink. It does make you feel self-conscious, yeah, especially now things are getting bigger and bigger. I find myself checking my flies when I go in, which I never used to do, because I know everyone will look at me.

'They forget that you make your money from having good hearing and you can hear the things they are whispering about you. We feel we have to be tactful. There's a guy I used to play with for six years who was telling me he can't get any gigs, that it was so hard. When he asked what I was up to I didn't want to tell him.'

Small wonder Danny felt uncomfortable: The Script were doing very well for themselves. The *Irish Examiner* later that month reported that the cash at two firms controlled by its members had increased sevenfold to €2.2 million. Accounts lodged by Madnotes Entertainment to Companies House in Britain show cash rose from £84,266 (€104,333) to £988,735 in the 12 months to the end of March 2011. Accumulated profits had risen more than sevenfold from £60,394 to £428,741. At Madnotes Publishing, a second company, cash increased from £169,148 to £824,704.

The band's hard-earned financial comfort didn't make them immune to the misfortunes of others, however. While on the road in the US in November, The Script were overcome when they watched TV reports of people grappling with their losses in the devastation left by Hurricane Sandy. It hit particularly close to home when they saw that New York's Long Island, where they were scheduled to play in early December, was one of the areas most severely hit. Glen has family who live there.

The band decided they had to do something to help and donated all the proceeds from the show's ticket sales, merchandise (a special T-shirt was created for the event) and even their fee to the Long Island Red Cross to aid the relief efforts. 'How could we rest when so many were in such need?' Danny asked *Billboard*. 'America has been so good to us and has enabled us to have a global career. We felt we had to do something to show our appreciation and give back and help. We hope that by stepping forward, others will do the same. And, we hope we [brought] some much-needed fun and enabled the people dealing with such a loss to escape and enjoy themselves for a bit.'

A little over a week into 2013 Danny was thrilled to learn that the band had been nominated for a Brit Award on 20 February. The band were in the running for best International Group along with The Killers, The Black Keys, Alabama Shakes and Fun, but Danny was realistic about their chances of winning at the London ceremony.

'We are not the type of band that wins, we've never been,' he told the *Daily Mirror*. 'I know I can't win the category. I've said we've been going for four years without getting recognised but you know, it's never stopped us and it's never taken us down a peg. We haven't won any awards and it doesn't bother us but being nominated and getting a pat on the back from the industry is great.'

'I was talking to a lot of people when I was on holiday over Christmas and it seems the more awards you get the more complacent you start to become,' he added to the *Daily Star*. 'We've always been pipped at it for whatever reason but it's never stopped us from going on and being successful.

'The stage we're at now – "Hall of Fame" has gone platinum in America, we're number one in Germany – I say don't give us the award, give it to someone who is more deserving, a younger band who need the help. We don't need the help. Finally we've got a bit of recognition – but we're rocking and rolling with or without awards.

'I haven't a clue if they're going to let us perform. That's why I went along to the launch last week – to press palms, apply some pressure and get somebody in a headlock. But seriously, we had a fantastic year in 2012 and it's just nice to get the nod.'

If the nomination represented Lady Luck smiling on them, the band then suffered a really bizarre run of bad luck in a matter of days in January. First a fire scare saw them evacuated from their hotel in Germany, then a day later dates of their European tour were put in jeopardy after heavy snowfall and blizzards. Then, on top of it all, Danny fractured his ribs after falling off an inflatable banana boat ride on holiday,

'I came off the back of an inflatable boat being towed by another boat,' he told the *Sun*. 'I was bouncing around on the fucking thing and I popped out the back and crashed on to my ribs. I can't take deep breaths to sing or have sex. I don't have a girlfriend to complain, though.'

CHAPTER 15

A WINNING VOICE

Perhaps it was a deliberate ploy to add to the tension and drama? Or maybe Danny and his fellow coaches on *The Voice* really did have their doubts over returning after just one series. Either way it got the show talked about in the press between seasons. In late August 2012 it was unofficially confirmed that Danny was signing up for a second series.

Like the Duracell bunny he is, he couldn't resist excitedly telling reporters how much he loved the show and had made real friends with his co-stars. 'I'm over the moon that Jessie will be back for a second series,' he told the *People*. 'We have a great friendship. Jessie wasn't a diva at all. It's really easy to put the crown of diva on whoever the biggest female singer is at the time. The Jessie I know isn't the one I read about.'

'I loved the first series. The experience itself was incredible,' he added to *Wales on Sunday*. 'I'd never been on TV doing anything like this before, so just to do that was a big thing for me. But the response we got was immense.

'It was the biggest launch for an entertainment show in the history of British television, which I think is phenomenal. And for the first four weeks, we were getting 14 million watching, which was incredible. The BBC are so proud of it, I'm so proud of it. I just loved the buzz about it. It shook up the establishment that was already there, which was needed.'

Danny said that the four coaches shared a unique chemistry so there was no need to change the dynamic. 'It's a weird thing because it sounds like a car crash when you say you're going to put those four artists together on a panel,' he joked. 'It sounds like a skit from *The Simpsons* or something. But I thought we worked brilliantly together.'

Danny maintained that Sir Tom Jones still impressed him the most, not just with his singing voice and famous friends but also his drinking prowess. 'I know lots of people use the word legend around him but he's more than that,' Danny told *Wales on Sunday*. 'I was lucky to spend a lot of time with him. People can go to a show for one night and see him, but not many people can say I got to hang out with him for eight weeks, which was great because you get the insight, you get to see what he's like when the camera's off – and he's just a gentleman, a really nice guy.

'He's always been on the forefront of my musical taste. He's always made brilliant albums and come back storming with whatever he does. And then he goes on a show that many people thought he might have been a little too old for and he goes on to win the show.'

Unsurprisingly, it seems the Irishman and the Welshman spent quite some time in the pub. 'It sounds like a start of a good joke, doesn't it?' laughed Danny. 'Of course, we had a few beers. It's the initiation with Sir Tom, isn't it? I don't think you get to talk to him properly if you haven't been anointed, so to speak.

'The very first night we all actually met, we all went out for dinner together, and lo and behold who were the last two at the bar? It was me and Tom. Will and Jessie had gone home and we were at the bar drinking and drinking, and he was telling me these incredible stories about Elvis and all the amazing times he's had and things that he'd done. I wish Elvis was still around so I could verify the stories with him, because some of them are just amazing.

'He comes from a day and age where you could be just be nice and calm and cool. Nowadays everyone is looking at the stars on the television and thinking I need to be more extravagant, or I need to be more extrovert than Lady Gaga. But all Tom needed was his voice – that was it. What I learned from him was how to conduct yourself in the industry.

'The legacy that he's left behind is what I'd love to achieve as well. Me and you are talking about him, but he is just a man, although we both acknowledge there is something special about him. He will go down in history as an absolute legend. How he conducts himself is a lesson to us. He has no airs or graces. The bigger the star the nicer they are and he epitomises that.

'Like I say, I hope they have me back. Apparently they had more people editing out my curses than trying to fix the chairs to make sure they turned around.'

Contracts had still to be signed by the start of September but Danny was fully committed to the show. 'I think they were worried about *The Voice*,' he said to *Daily Star Sunday* of *The X Factor*. 'They endlessly slagged us, so I find it incredibly satisfying they have now taken on contestants playing instruments and real artists like we do.'

Danny told the same newspaper that there would be a lot of changes to improve the second series, including more blind auditions as that aspect of the show pulled in more viewers. 'The four coaches and the BBC know what to do to make sure this series is even better than the first one,' he said. 'We all agreed we need to get the songs and the artists out sooner. We were all throwing ideas down on the table and talked about writing a song for the winner to release as soon as the show finishes.'

Songs would now be available to download on the same night to create both a buzz and a back catalogue for the artists. Another twist would see coaches able to steal acts from each other later on in the run.

They wanted to reinvigorate the format, but Danny was adamant that this wouldn't mean trying to put on an act. He wasn't about to try to ape Simon Cowell with a Mr Nasty role. 'I was just brought on to be me,' he said. 'I can't do it. I can't stand there and give a person bad news in a bad way – I just am that way personally. I'm not hired to be an actor, so you're just going to get me – you know, the same emotional, jumping up on the chair Danny.'

Filming started at Manchester's MediaCityUK the week before Christmas and producers said a massive 30,000 people had signed up for the blind auditions this year. Danny was proud that the feedback from the first series showed that having a rock band member on the show was inspiring a new generation of kids to take up instruments.

'After *The Voice*, kids were coming up to me and saying, "I learned to play guitar like you did on the U2 tune" or "I learned piano like you played on that song,"' he told the *Irish Sun*. 'It would have been a crime not to have someone from a band up there – not just for us to get more recognition, but for bands in general. Bands aren't getting played on radio the way they used to, especially guitar-playing bands.'

By January the blind auditions had been filmed and Danny was full of praise for the new format. 'When it comes to the chop, when I am down to six at the knockout stages, I can lose an artist but I can also take someone else's,' he told the *Sun*. 'There will be a lot more opportunities to battle. I'm loving it – it's gloves off. We just go straight in.'

The new series also meant he and Tom could enjoy

drinking together again. 'We've been all hanging out backstage and Tom – I'm not going to lie, he drank me under the table on more than one occasion,' he told the same newspaper. 'Yeah man, five bottles of champagne at six o'clock in the morning – I didn't know he was still able to do it. We were staying in a hotel and I made a mistake: I tried to leave the room before a bottle was empty. Tom just clicked his fingers and said, "Sit back down."'

In between the blind auditions and filming the live shows, it was back to business for The Script. They played the European leg of their world tour, which had begun the previous September, including a return to Dublin – this time for five cut-price concerts at the very end of February. Mindful of the crippling effects the recession on their homeland, the band slashed their ticket prices to €39.50 for Dublin's O2 and naturally it sold out, although it probably would have anyway.

As always, the band stopped for pictures and autographs for the dedicated members of The Script Family – fans who wait for hours after their shows. Danny even handed out tea and blankets to fans in rainy Nottingham. As one fan said, 'You don't get many bands or celebs doing something like that.'

The Script – and Mark in particular – were enjoying success after working so hard to establish themselves. But they were enjoying it sensibly. All the time they had been carefully and cleverly considering their career and investing shrewdly in their businesses – and banking more all the time. The *Irish Examiner* revealed on 5 March that

Danny and Mark's Madnotes Publishing Ltd and Madnotes Entertainment Ltd had made combined profits for 2012 totalling £711,386. The combined cash pile at the firms totalled £1.72million.

Looking at the two firms individually, accounts filed with Companies House in the UK showed that accumulated profits at Madnotes Publishing Ltd had increased by £410,624 to £561,989 in the 12 months to the end of 30 April 2012, and that the firm's cash pile at the end of April was £735,002. Meanwhile accounts for Madnotes Entertainment Ltd showed its accumulated profits had jumped by £300,762 to £729,503, and the firm's cash pile totalled £985,003.

The directors and shareholders of the two firms are the founding members of The Script, Danny and Mark. Madnotes Publishing Ltd made advances of £365,800 to Mark during the year with him repaying £362,800. Advances of £365,800 were made to Danny during the year with him repaying £414,510 – Danny had owed the firm £50,800 at the start of the year.

As Danny set about talking up the new series beforehand in press interviews, he said the quality of the contestants for the second series had passed that of the first and told more Tom Jones stories.

'What do we talk about? Oh, you don't talk to Tom Jones. You just shut up and listen,' he said to *Mail Online*. 'If you're lucky he starts singing to you. The best bit is when you're drinking with him, and it's at that stage of the night when hotel staff are putting the breakfast things out and he's singing lines from songs. It's like poetry. We must have had about four drinking sessions during the last series, and I'm talking drinking sessions – four or five bottles rather than a glass of champagne.'

Despite headlines over falling viewing figures as the series progressed, Danny said he was delighted by the response to *The Voice*. 'Absolutely,' he stressed. 'The fact that we went up against a big juggernaut like *Britain's Got Talent* and gave viewers something different – I think it was great. And remember, we're not an entertainment show. We aren't a circus. We don't have dancing dogs. We have real singers who are trying to make it in the industry.

'The bosses have looked at how things can be improved and come up with a new element called The Steal. The judges can steal other judges' acts they want to save – which is what happens in the real music industry. When a judge rejects an act, the rest of us are allowed to take them on. In this business, one man's trash is another man's treasure.'

Will.i.am revealed that he'd wanted to sign up to the second series of *The Voice* as soon as he knew Danny was returning. 'The fact is, the first two people who said they were coming back were me and Danny,' he told *BANG Showbiz* at the series launch. 'I didn't wait. After the last taping I was like, "So what are you going to do next year? Are you going to do it again?" He was like, "Hell yeah." And I was like, "Me too." On the day of the last show I knew I wanted to come back.'

Danny told the *Daily Star* in March that the extra

profile on *The Voice* was responsible for a happy by-product on tour – female fans flashing their breasts at gigs. 'There's a few flashers now who wait till the last song and get their boobs out,' he said. 'You feel like you let your hair down emotionally – that's what a Script gig is like.'

While Danny put his hand in his pocket and sponsored co-star Jessie J's brave move to shave her head for Comic Relief, he also let her and *The Voice* host Holly Willoughby wax his chest for the charity. 'It didn't take long,' he said. 'In fairness that's not a bad trade-off, getting your hair ripped off by those two hotties.'

At the same time as the pre-recorded episodes hit the TV screens, The Script were finishing off the UK leg of their tour, and Danny told *The Times* he was far from exhausted juggling both. 'No,' he said, 'I'm the hardest-working man in show business. Not really but ... people say they want to be me and I have one answer for them: work as hard as I do and see where it gets you, then come and tell me what you want to do.

'I know if you are beamed into people's sitting rooms on a Saturday night you can't really get upset when people recognise you. You become public property I guess, part of the family. And if that means I appeal to all ages then I'm happy about that.'

Unlike the first series, Danny was single – and said his newfound TV fame as 'that bloke sitting next to Tom Jones' was making him a hit with the ladies. 'Being on TV is like an accelerator,' he told the *Sun*. 'The girls in the street that would pass you by are the same girls stopping and going fanatical over you. And you get a real kick out of it. Do I kiss the girls? Of course I do. I'm a living, breathing man. If I weren't in the public eye I wouldn't get the same action I do now – I've got a face like a foot.'

Danny was back on *The Voice* having just finished a UK tour, and admitted that being on the road was easier when he didn't have someone back home. 'It was like I was leaving half of myself behind,' he told the *Sun*. 'So being single for the past year has been really liberating – I'm definitely mingling.

'We definitely get up to some rock star antics – we just don't take them to VIP spots where people can take a picture of you. We embarrass ourselves behind closed doors rather than in public. Some artists call photographers to take pictures of them falling out of clubs. That's the last thing I want to see the next morning.'

But despite enjoying the company of his fans, Danny admitted that all the attention could be a bit intense. 'I'll wake up in the morning and there'll be 30 girls outside the bus wanting to take photos with me,' he said. 'But it's not like these women are cockroaches, they're welcome. And half of them will be really good-looking. We've been blessed with great fans in that respect.

'I remember this one show – I look out at the front row and there are these girls in Danny masks with their tops off. It was the scariest thing I've ever seen. We get a lot of knickers thrown on stage too – I could give Tom Jones a run for his money.'

Mention of the Welshman brought the talk back to *The Voice* and Danny went on to lambast *The X Factor*, labelling it as is cruel and superficial. 'I know they're both singing competitions but *The Voice* is a very different show. We don't make fools of people,' he told the *Sun*. '*The X Factor* shows more of the acts we're supposed to laugh at than acts with genuine talent. I watched some of the last series of *The X Factor* but I had to turn off when they were laughing at this dude. When you have thousands of people booing some poor sod on stage, that has the cringe factor.'

Danny was certain that the tweaks to the format would set the shows apart even more. 'We're no fools. We know the "blinds" were the most exciting part of last year so there have been tiny tinkers … we've learned a lot. We're getting tighter as a unit but at the same time it's getting more competitive. There's more slagging going on.'

Occasionally Danny had amused himself during the blind auditions by trying to guess what the singers looked like, jotting down predictions such as 'slim, brown hair, funny dress' in his notepad while they were singing, insisting: 'I can hear it in the voice!'

But there was one starlet he could never have predicted. When the first episode of the second series aired at the end of March, there was defining moment for Danny: the truly heartwarming and inspirational audition of 26-year-old Andrea Begley from Pomeroy, Co Tyrone. After losing practically all of her sight from glaucoma as a child, she was 90 per cent blind but had the voice of an angel – and she had Danny enthralled from the start.

Fittingly, she sang 'Angel' by Sarah McLachlan but so poor is her sight – essentially only recognising some shapes close up – she had no idea whether any of the judges had even turned for her or not. Danny was the first, telling her: 'That was absolutely beautiful.

'From the first line of that song I just knew that this was something special,' he went on. 'The mood just changed in the room. That is what a megastar does. They just change it. It was a great moment. The emotion that you sang with is the same emotion that I've strived myself to try and get and to look for in other artists. I'd be in the arms of an angel if you were on my team.'

When Andrea admitted she was not entirely sure whether anyone turned round or not, Danny jumped up on stage to give her a hug and assured her: 'The whole of the UK just turned round.'

After much to-ing and fro-ing between Sir Tom and Danny, Andrea decided to go for Danny, but she made sure she thanked Tom for turning around.

Andrea – a niece of Irish country music star Philomena Begley – said: 'In the past, when I've entered competitions, the feedback was always that I could have moved about more or had a bit more stage presence, which is obviously difficult when you are visually impaired. The big pull for me with *The Voice* is the style of the show – the blind audition. They could not see me and I could not see them so that made me feel equal to them. For once I was being judged solely on my singing. Some people are good at dancing and performing. I'm not a performer, for me it's all about the singing and the vocal, so this was the right thing for me. The judges could focus on my singing without any of the other distractions.

'My parents have always motivated me and tried to encourage me to achieve as much as I could. I'm very ambitious and I don't want this to hold me back.'

Afterwards she said to *Sunday Life*: 'It is unbelievable and I am so excited. I really admire The Script and Danny's songwriting style. I went to their concert in Belfast, but never thought in a million years that I would end up working with Danny.'

Andrea then revealed that she had picked him as her coach to help her develop her songwriting skills. 'Danny is a pleasure to work with and just so easy to get along with,' she told the *Irish Daily Mail*. 'He is a helpful mentor and interested in me and is willing to share his insight and experiences.

'He also gave me a pep talk on where you can go wrong quickly – for someone like me starting out in the music business that is invaluable. That advice will stay with me outside of *The Voice* and proves that I definitely made the right decision when it came to choosing my coach.'

Danny declared that he meant business this time round: 'This year I'm not settling for anything other than winning.' His team was starting to shape up nicely with the addition of Nadeem Leigh, who spoke movingly on the show about his battle with alcohol and drug addiction, as well as the loss of his 37-year-old mother Deborah, who died after having a stroke when he was 19.

'I've been waiting for Nadeem to come along,' Danny said after the audition. 'The rest of them have been great singers and they've got a great vibe which I could possibly coach but he was magic, magic.'

Danny told *Glamour* magazine in April that he was also on the prowl for a new lover – but one who was secure in herself. 'I just got out of a long-distance relationship and although I'm not with that person now, that comes with its own heartache.

'I have the freedom to travel and have my heart with me. It's hard to keep a woman's mind at ease when you're away and she thinks you're always out at a party. I tend to not go for insecure women. There's no bigger turn-off than a girl who says, "What are you doing in the studio? You should be here with me." That means they don't get what I need to live. I'm at the age where I get that you don't need to be together all the time to make something work.

'I like a woman with a bit more meat on her' he added. 'And I love women with tattoos. I'm a tattoo whore.'

Winning female attention had always come easy, he said, but it was not always the attention he was looking for. 'I once had two mums and their daughters come to a meet and greet,' he told the magazine. 'The daughters weren't interested, but at 2am the mothers were outside our hotel rooms, trying to get in.'

At the same time The Script – with Mark the driving

force – was expanding its businesses, setting up its own management and publishing company to nurture talent as Danny was finding it on *The Voice*. 'It's baby steps,' said Mark. 'We're not trying to do anything crazy but we're taking on a couple of little projects that we're really excited about. To be able to bring new bands on tour with us or get them on stage during soundcheck is a nice thing.'

'We have eight hours a day to sit around and talk shit,' Danny added. 'We can waffle on about the industry and music and how we can improve things.'

It was an important point, as Danny and the other coaches were forced to bat back media claims that their contestants on *The Voice* were suffering because of the judges' jet-set lifestyles, touring commitments and so on. 'I am always available to coach and mentor my acts, even when I am abroad with mobile, internet etc,' emphasised Danny, who had been on tour in Australia in early April. 'I am still working with Max from the last series and I've written and recorded songs for Bo's new album which is out soon.'

In April, he admitted to *Mail on Sunday's You* magazine he wasn't necessarily the best singer in the world, but he was on the show to represent all the people who play an instrument and want to rock out. 'We've seen more people turn up with guitars or playing the piano, and I love that,' he said. 'Bands don't get to showcase themselves on TV very often these days. It's not fashionable: bookers are more likely to spend a fortune on Beyoncé or Justin Timberlake.'

He told the same magazine that he is at his happiest when he is 'in the studio, writing and performing songs. I love those padded walls. That's where I'm comfortable.' But he also revealed what makes pains him: each year he visits sick children in hospital and has to see the suffering they endure. 'I've started a tradition of going to the Temple Street Children's Hospital in Dublin every Christmas,' he revealed. 'That makes me really sad, but it's nice to know you can put a smile on the children's faces for a little while.'

There were still tour dates in the Far East and Australasia to honour before *The Voice* live shows and then the festival circuit after that. Danny told Singapore newspaper *The New Paper* that when the band first got going, they spent hours writing songs and fine-tuning them in the studio, only dreaming of going on tour. Here they were now, in huge demand the world over, selling out tours – but that meant it was hard to get the time to work on new material. 'Now we're touring so much, it's rare that we're in one place just to write,' he said.

The only solution was to write while on tour: 'We never stop writing and we do that when we have some down time. It felt just like yesterday when we were sitting with our fingers crossed, not knowing how our album would do. And now we are in Singapore. We're blessed, it's been an absolute dream.'

After The Script played in the Philippines in April, Danny unwittingly became involved in a love triangle. Miss Universe runner-up Janine Tugonon revealed she had broken up with boyfriend Jaypee Santos after a year because she had fallen in love with Danny. The Filipino beauty queen shocked her country after admitting on TV she had become attracted to the singer after meeting him backstage at a gig. During their time backstage, Danny told the 23-year-old to follow him on Twitter and he would follow back – which led to them starting to talk.

Janine – who was first runner-up at Miss Universe 2012 – revealed her boyfriend went mad after discovering they had been texting each other. 'Honestly, we're not currently on good terms,' she said. 'I said to him I needed some time to think.'

She tried to calm the outrage in the Philippines by insisting nothing was 'going on' and told snipers to 'stop jumping to conclusions'.

Her boyfriend Jaypee, a software engineer, weighed in on Twitter to claim it was 'just a time of confusion' for Janine and insisted, in a series of posts, that the 'other guy issue has now stopped' and that they were 'still talking and trying to fix this mess'.

During her TV interview, Janine revealed a bit more about the tangled mess. 'Since I know the staff at the venue, I told them I am a hyper fan of The Script and [asked] could I be able to meet him? So I met him and Jaypee was there. I introduced him because Danny asked, "Do you have a boyfriend?" I said, "Yeah, that's my boyfriend." Then he said, "Follow me on Twitter and I will follow you back." I took up the offer and direct messaged him.'

It was because she did not reveal the nature of the messages that her boyfriend was not happy. Apparently Jaypee told Janine if she really wasn't interested in the singer, then she wouldn't have communicated with him. The pair then argued and decided to end their relationship.

At the same time, and as if he had learnt nothing with the drama with Bo, Danny had the eye for another contestant in the new series of *The Voice*: former *Hollyoaks* actress Alice Barlow, who played Rae Wilson in the TV soap up to 2011. 'She's a lovely-looking girl,' he remarked to his fellow coaches about the 21-year-old blonde, with Jessie teasing him about how often he gets distracted by the appearance of the contestants. 'I don't think there is a red-blooded man in the world who wouldn't find her attractive,' he retorted.

'I'm a ladies' man,' he told the *Sun*. 'There are a lot of pretty girls on the show. I'm telling them they are gorgeous because I am single and I am looking! I wouldn't rule out dating a fan or a contestant. Ever!'

Alice Barlow said he gave her lots of advice after she joined Team Danny. 'It was really flattering, especially from Danny. He's a good-looking man but I have a boyfriend. It felt very surreal,' she told the *Liverpool Echo*. 'It was amazing to meet and work with him. He's a lovely guy and he always made me feel comfortable. I really connected with him. He understood me and what it was like to be in the public eye. He told me what I needed to improve on and he gave me lots of advice, mainly to come out of my shell and show people who I am.'

'I love The Script so that's another reason why I chose Danny.'

Danny, meanwhile, revealed his fellow coach Sir Tom Jones had given him pulling tips: 'Tom just says, "Be cool and shut up!" I think I ruin my chances by opening my mouth and letting it run. But as soon as Tom switches it on, all the girls head over to him.'

Danny also admitted to the *Daily Star* he would have no qualms about using the show to try to find a date. 'I am single and I am looking,' he said. 'There have been some lovely-looking girls on the show. The others have said "Danny's using the show as his own Take Me Out" which is true, but the thing is I can't fucking see them until I turn the chair round.'

Maybe women might not be so quick to take him up on his offers if they knew the secret nickname his band-mates have for him because of his Man v Food binges. 'They call me Danny Dustbin when I'm on tour in the US,' the singer says. 'I love the food challenges and can stick plenty away.'

Singer Dido was on hand to help out Danny in the battle rounds and his charges were full of praise for his coaching on the show.

'Out of all the coaches he's the most hands-on,' said Paul Carden. 'We're quite close in age so we've got a lot in common – apart from he's got more money.'

'There's a sense of family in Team Danny,' Nadeem

added. 'We all get on really well, but the experience of working with Danny and Dido has been very personal. It's been mind-blowing.'

Danny was overcome when he had to deal with the heartbreak of losing his acts as the battle rounds drew to a close, knowing there was little chance of a lifeline. Viewers saw Danny crumble when he faced choosing between Nadeem Leigh and Karl Michael to decide who survived in the contest. After hearing them go head-to-head performing Daniel Merriweather's 'Red', Danny had tears in his eyes. 'All I asked for was emotion,' he said as he opted for Karl. 'And you gave that and so much more. I'm an idiot for putting you together.'

The stakes had been high for both contestants. Karl had already been an artist, recording in New York, but had failed in his attempt at stardom, becoming a window cleaner in defeat. Nadeem had also been a struggling musician and saw *The Voice* as a last shot, having previously found music as the outlet to get clean in his struggle with drug addiction.

'When I put them together I didn't realise how good Nadeem is,' Danny said. 'But I know Karl. Around the piano he is incredible.'

With the choices of Abi Sampa, Alex Buchanan, Andrea Begley, Conor Scott, Karl Michael, Mitchel Emms and Sean Rumsey, Team Danny became complete.

Things got heated at the end of May when viewers saw Danny call will.i.am 'a fucking idiot'. And after one decision, Will exclaimed: 'What the fuck?'

Speaking about Danny, Will said: 'I got offended when he recently called me a fucking idiot. That was not cool. I told him.'

As the competition approached its climax, Danny chose his three – Andrea Begley, Mitchell Emms and Karl Michael. But things took a surreal twist for Danny when he had to perform in front of Britain's most famous VIP – The Queen.

Her Majesty was officially opening the BBC's revamped state-of-the-art Broadcasting House in London and was treated to a special performance by The Script and Indiana (a BBC Introducing artist) of the David Bowie song 'Heroes'. Afterwards, Danny described the experience as 'bizarre' and 'pretty intimidating'.

'It was crazy,' he told the *Sun* later. 'We played in the Live Lounge by Royal request. She asked for us – I didn't think the Queen was rocking The Script! She enjoyed the performance. It was like an out-of-body experience for me.'

After they'd played 'Heroes', the Queen chatted with them. 'She said, "Great performance," Danny revealed. 'There was a girl called Indiana who was performing with us. We were explaining this will be her start (in the industry) and that she'll end up at Glastonbury one day. The Queen said, "Glastonbury – that's the place with all the mud, isn't it?" And I said, "In fairness, if you wanted to go down, you'd probably have to put on the Royal wellies." It was hilarious.

'And she said, "I don't know why they don't just move

the date." People have been trying to figure out for ages how you get around the mud – and the Queen just figured out the answer.'

The band had known they were to play to a special guest but weren't told who until five days before. Danny said he was 'almost stuck to the floor with fear' when he met the Queen. 'When I found out it was the Queen I thought it was very strange they had chosen us but a massive compliment.

'She's one terrific lady,' he added.

Back in Ireland those comments would see Danny and the band targeted by internet trolls, who branded them 'Union Jack bastards'. Danny made a mature move to turn the vitriol on its head by saying they refused to live in the past.

'Irish people have a stigma where we get drinks and shillelaghs pinned to us everywhere we go,' he told the *Irish Mirror*. 'But we want to represent modern Ireland. We are not chewing over old stuff – we are looking to the future. I thought I wasn't going to be an ignorant little bollocks about it. We had been requested by the Queen personally to do this. We're supposed to be ambassadors for the youth of Ireland so we went and did it, showcasing Ireland and Irish music – the way we do around the world and U2 did before us.

'We were tweeted afterwards by crazies calling us "Union Jack bastards" and loyalists. But we did it to show we represent modern Ireland – in the spirit of a new relationship between Britain and Ireland.'

Back on *The Voice*, Mitchell broke down in tears as he was knocked out and hugged Danny, who told the audience: 'All I know is that there are record companies all across the UK right now that are going to snap him up. I absolutely know it.'

But Danny also fired a word of warning ahead of the semi-finals with the news that last year's winner, Leanne Mitchell, had only sold 895 copies of her newly released debut album. 'That's not my fault, that's not the show's fault, that's not the BBC's fault.' This year's artists, he told the *Sun*, needed to do more to make the most of the opportunity the show was affording them. 'There are some amazing singers on the show,' he said. 'But although they have a great skill, that's the tip of the iceberg. It's about how well rounded they are. We only get to sing for about five per cent of our careers. The rest of it is how you conduct yourself, your plans.

'The misconception is that it's up to me to make my acts famous, but we're not a record company. We don't have loads of money to be throwing around on acts. Universal are the ones with the contracts. We set up the platform and give them their own lane into the industry, but at the end of the day it's up to the person themselves. None of us got here because a label threw money at us.'

On 15 June four acts made it one step closer to their dream. Andrea Begley made it through to the final for Danny, along with Matt Henry, Leah McFall and Mike Ward.

The next big event for The Script was headlining

Britain's Isle of Wight festival, but Mark and Glen said Danny was now too well known to enjoy the festivities. 'We feel sorry for him, you know,' Mark told Absolute Radio. 'We can go out into the festival, get some food and go out on some of the rides but Danny wouldn't be able to do that.

'He's been catapulted into the limelight. He really can't go anywhere. I almost hate going to the local (pub) with him. He often turns to disguises. He's got this flat cap that he wears a lot but that doesn't work. He's like Godzilla – he's too tall.'

Danny flew his finalist Andrea with them by helicopter to the Isle of Wight to give her a taste of the big time but also to help promote her ahead of the final. Now, on the eve of the big night, Danny invited the *Sun* to join them at their last-minute rehearsals, where she sang the Evanescence track 'My Immortal' and Sarah McLachlan's 'Angel' before joining The Script for 'Hall of Fame'.

'Isn't that gorgeous?' Danny said. 'Andrea sounds her best when there's silence around her – when it sounds like she could be in a bar. I'd be a fool to go against the odds – Leah has an amazing chance of winning. But there will hopefully be a few extra million people watching the final. Those people will get to experience Andrea for the first time, and you can't underestimate the power of a great song in the hands of a great singer. When she sang 'Angel' at her audition, there wasn't anyone in here who wasn't crying. It's not over until it's over and I wouldn't bet against Andrea.

'At this stage, nobody could say she is in the final due to sympathy. People don't pick up the phone to vote because you are blind. Andrea has fought for this the entire way. She has put in the hours because she knows hard work pays off and I'd love to see her win the show. Either way we have a plan – if she wins or doesn't win.'

But win she did at the final on 22 June, much to the shock of many as her fellow countrywoman Leah McFall on Team Will had been favourite. Andrea told viewers it was a victory she said she 'never, ever, ever could have imagined' was possible. 'I actually can't speak,' she said. 'I never ever, ever could have imagined this. Hopefully I'll try my best to put your vote to good use and be a success.'

Danny told the audience just how proud he was of his protégé: 'It just proves that a great, great singer with a great song, you can knock down walls. You can smash down anything they put in front of you,' he said.

After her rendition of 'My Immortal', Danny said: 'There wasn't one hair on my body that wasn't standing up.' Turning to Andrea, he added: 'You're an inspiration to me. I've learned more from you than you have from me.'

During the grand final, the 2013 victor took to the stage with The Script to perform 'Hall of Fame', which she said was 'such an honour' and 'such a privilege'. Afterwards, Andrea revealed, Danny had suggested they work on a track together. 'He has expressed an interest in writing with me,' she said. 'And I'd love it to happen. I feel like there are a lot of opportunities.'

Danny added: 'We'll have an album out before Christmas. I'm excited about people hearing her songs. She has two hits songs already from what I've heard. I'd love to work with Andrea going forward – if she'll have me.'

But will.i.am was taken aback by the surprise result. Not long after Andrea was announced as the winner, he tweeted: 'You should feel the audience's vibration in the room tonight after the public vote ... its #unexplainable ... so sad ... #perplexed.' He quickly followed that with a second tweet: 'Andrea is amazing ... #dontGETmeWRONG ... but we know who has the incredible #voice.'

Commenting on his controversial tweets, Andrea told the Press Association: 'I had a good chat with Will afterwards. Every coach is 110 per cent behind their act and Will was definitely very much from the get-go behind Leah, and I'm not surprised that he said that. He actually said to me that had I been on his team he'd have the same level of support for me. It's his act. He wants to support them all the way, and I have no doubt beyond the show Leah will do exceptionally well. She will be very successful.

'Will wishes me well, but obviously everybody wants their act to win and I can understand that he maybe was disappointed. But at the end of the day the audience voted for me, so that's it.'

Andrea also revealed that special advice from her mentor and his band had helped her to overcome any nerves on the night and secure victory. 'Before the final began, the guys from The Script took me aside and told me they still get nervous before gigs,' she said. 'But they told me to just go out and enjoy it and block everything else out, so that's what I did.'

In fact, as Andrea told *Metro*, she had enjoyed a great relationship with Danny throughout the series and counted him as a friend. 'Danny and myself just always totally got along like good friends,' she said. 'It was always fun chatting, and with the Irish sense of humour. He has spoken to me and said he really wants to be involved so I am very happy to have him on board.'

'There were so many great moments on the show,' Andrea added to the *Belfast Telegraph*, 'but the biggest highlight for me has to be my performance with The Script. I've always been a fan. I've gone to their concerts and listened to their songs on my iPod, but never in a million years did I think I'd be performing on stage with them. It's something I'll always treasure.

'Danny is so nice and down to earth. From the get-go he understood the direction I needed to go in as an artist. I write my own songs too and he has really supported my original material and wants to be involved with my new album. Having Danny on board would be immense. I know he's got his own commitments with The Script – I think they're recording at the moment too – so I don't expect him to give me all of his time. I'd just be so happy to have him involved in whatever way he can.'

Danny had finished the series a winner – the perfect

opportunity to bow out on a high. He initially said he wanted to return to defend his crown, but the truth was that the double-jobbing was taking its toll on the band. It had only ever been supposed to help the band in the first place, and they all knew it couldn't be allowed to take away from their music.

'It got tough this year,' Danny admitted afterwards. 'One weekend we had two festivals, a live show and three rehearsals – it was hard going.'

'Normally for musicians it's burning out from coke binges,' Mark added. 'He's actually burnt out because he's working hard.'

Summing up his time on *The Voice*, Danny told the *Sun*: 'It has been a real gift. We're classed as alternative rock, but we've never wanted to stay under the radar with a niche following. There's nothing precious about us at all – and we certainly don't expect everyone who likes us to be wearing skinny jeans. I've always wanted to reach as many people as possible with my music. Whether that's teenagers or parents on the school run, it really doesn't matter to me.'

CHAPTER 16

THE DANNY
WE KNOW

Danny seems to be universally loved by those in the music business who have encountered him, from fellow musicians to radio disc jockeys. I asked some music industry professionals what they thought makes Danny special as an artist.

Ralph McLean is an award-winning BBC TV and radio presenter, with his own Radio Ulster show. He says that while Danny is the focal point of The Script, it is his friendship and teamwork with his band-mates that make them so successful as one entity. 'Danny is the lightning rod, if you like. With a quiff like that and the good looks, could he be anything else? But Glen and Mark are just as important in terms of band dynamics. They are tight as musicians but tighter as friends. That's rare in this business. Danny may do most of the interviews but they're a unit. You don't play together since 2001 and not build a bond that's deeper than the surface crap of TV fame and fortune.'

Ralph believes that much of The Script's success lies in the fact that they are genuine friends, and not some manufactured act. 'First and foremost they are a band in the proper sense of the term,' he says. 'They don't have that fabricated, formulated feel that many pop acts have. You don't feel they were glued together in some faceless record company boardroom by some evil overlord in ill-fitting trousers. They are mates together doing their thing whether you like it or not. Like all good bands should be.

'The "us versus them" vibe is important. That builds over years of no success. It grounds the group. Years of playing toilets to little or no reaction, and sneering critical swipes as well, hardens a band and you can see that in The Script. They're enjoying their success but not dazzled by it. They've seen too much of the tough side of the business to buy into the glamour and glitz bullshit. Unlike most "pop" acts, The Script feel like a "band" not a product. That's an enormous credit to them.'

Ralph also firmly believes that The Script have the blueprint for continued global success. Their music is so well crafted that they can go from strength to strength. 'As a band they've got all it takes to deliver the goods on a global scale,' he says. 'They've probably always had it but now it feels honed to perfection.

'From the moment I heard their debut album I just knew they were going to be players on that big stage.

They had a sound that tapped into that so called "big" music that the likes of The Waterboys drew up the blueprints for and U2 then took to the bank. Vast, sweeping sentiment blended with Celtic melancholy and old-fashioned guitar pop hooks. Never underestimate Celtic melancholy! It's a universal thing to wallow in a little moody reflection and dejection.

'Add it to a big chorus or three and you're on your way! It's a potent mix. Add a good looking, enigmatic lead singer with plenty to say off mic and you've got a concoction that's got "next big thing" stamped all over it. Given that all those parts seemed in place so early, it's a bit surprising it took them so long really.'

Their fans – The Script Family – are of paramount importance to the trio, and that was something that struck Ralph from the very first moment he encountered the band live. 'I first saw the band in person backstage at a Children in Need TV gig at the Kings Hall complex in Belfast. They were only starting out really and quite far down a showbiz heavy line-up but I remember their performance – they really went for it and gave their all – and particularly how they handled themselves afterwards.

'While many a band and pampered performer shot off into the Belfast night, Danny and the boys stood signing autographs and chatting to the assembled throng by the front gates for ages. I was impressed by their attitude that night. Every fan was important to them and fans remember that kind of gesture. Loyalty is a big thing in pop and if you can get a young audience on your side from early on you're flying.'

For Ralph, it was 'The Man Who Can't Be Moved' that was their breakthrough song and set the template for the anthemic sound that would become their signature. 'That was the first Script track to get my attention,' he says. '"We Cry", the first single, passed me by for some reason.

'Big is the word that springs to mind with the band. That vast, anthemic stadium pomp was there from the off. It's rare that a band's sound is so surefooted from so early on. It was never going to win them cool points with the music press but you just knew it was destined to connect with audiences across the world. They always seemed very well fitted out for success. Those very earliest tracks clearly identified the band as contenders for that U2 crown. You could hear it in the sound and in the sentiment. This was big music built for stadiums.

'For me seeing the band support Paul McCartney at Shea Stadium in 2009 was a significant moment. When the fab one re-opened the stadium as the Citi Field he asked The Script to be his support act. That's an amazing honour and I'm sure the band felt the hand of history on their shoulder that night. When a Beatle asks for your services I think you can safely say you've made it.'

Ralph believes that the band have now reached a level that means true global success is attainable, due in no small part due to Danny's prowess as a frontman. 'Right now it feels like the world is ready for Danny and The

Script. They're holding all the cards and how far they push it all depends on how they play them.

'There's a great line of global success for bands like U2 that pump out proper stadium anthems that are tinged with Celtic sadness and a certain bittersweet beauty. The Script have that quality. They paint in broad strokes, which is something that all stadium bands have to do. They've got the necessary big chorus quality that all bands seeking to speak on the biggest stages simply have to master.

'Every night Danny gives himself over to the audience and all the greats from Bono down know you have to do that. You have to surrender to the fans. Give yourself up and let those people into your heart. He knows that and the band know it as well. Whether the cool kids like them or not, The Script are well on the way to being one of the biggest bands ever to come from this island and Danny one of the most significant front men ever to grace a stadium stage. Anyone who loves music here should be very proud of them.'

It was a calculated move when Danny went forward as a coach on *The Voice* and Ralph says it was the right business move to make. 'Some would say it's career suicide to appear on something like *The Voice*. It's a credibility bypass for many. Don't expect to be cool after you sign that contract, because once you're working for the man you'll never be remotely cool or credible ever again. I don't think that ever registered with Danny, though.

'Cool is not a word bandied about when The Script are mentioned. Like Snow Patrol before them, cool is something that just never happened for them anyway. If the intelligentsia are never going to fawn over you anyway, who cares about judging a pop show? Danny knows his young audience well. Cool is not what it's about. The audience that show opened him and his band's music up to is probably impossible to quantify.

'He may have signed a death warrant in terms of ever being cool but in terms of profile it sent him into the stratosphere. There's no way back from those heights if you hanker after acceptance in the *NME*, but if you want to be one of the biggest bands in the world, it's the right thing to do. When he looks at the band's tour schedule and the band's bank balance, I'm sure he sleeps easy!'

But Ralph also believes that because Danny's profile has grown to such an extent that it should see him strike out as a solo artist one day. 'Despite the band bond that clearly exists, a Danny solo career seems inevitable. Danny had that easy charm just dripping from him from the very first night I saw him perform. He also had that most elusive of attributes – presence. You can't buy it or fake it. When he walked in the green room that night he was a star. Regardless of record sales and all that peripheral stuff – and remember he was only starting out then – he made heads turn. Most importantly, he also knew how to handle it all. You can't put a price on that.'

Andrea Begley, as we know, won the second series of *The Voice* with Danny as her coach and has plans to work with him, something I asked her about in person in an interview at the *Sunday Life* offices in August 2013.

'We have been in touch with each other, we've been emailing each other, so hopefully he will be getting involved in some shape or form on the album, but obviously he has left the show now as well,' she said. 'The band are concentrating on their new album, so I know his time is very precious at the moment, but he has said that he's very keen to get involved, so we'll keep on staying in contact and hopefully we'll get something sorted in the near future.

'It's the label who carry it forward [after the show], but Danny made it clear from the get-go that he wanted to be involved. He can have a bit of input and the label are content for him to be involved, but he's got his commitments too, touring in America flat out, so he's been out of the country for quite some time.

'He did call me the Monday after I'd won on the Saturday and said, "Look, keep me posted on what happens" and as I say, we've been emailing each other and we've spoke a couple of times.'

Andrea says she would love the opportunity to work with Danny again, be that on their material, her own or as a support act on tour. 'You never know, we need to meet up and have a chat. Danny was always a great supporter of my own material especially and he would be keen to work with me on that, so I'm hoping that will happen, whether it be on this album or maybe in the future, fingers crossed.

'I'm a big fan of The Script's music. It's auto-biographical really, and my songwriting would be about life experiences. In terms of that sentiment it would be in a similar vein to theirs.'

Andrea also reiterated what a calming influence Danny had been ahead of the final, giving her the benefit of his years of experience. 'They [The Script] were all there at the final, as they were performing at it with me, and I said to them, "I'm absolutely shattered with nerves here. I really don't know how I'm going to get through this."

'Danny actually said to me that before they do shows and before they do festivals, they still get nervous. So it kinda made me feel a bit better, in the sense that if The Script still get nervous – and look how massive they are and how long they've been going – then it's all right for me to get nervous.

'His attitude was, "Well, look – you've got to this point. You achieved a lot to get to this stage, you just go out there and enjoy it. Whatever happens, happens. Let the audience make their mind up from that. Try and get out there and relax more and enjoy it, and the more you do that, the better your performance will be."

'I don't know how or why it quite happened, or what switch flipped on the night – obviously I was very nervous – but I managed to be able to hold it together and not let the nerves cripple me. That was an achievement in itself. I was happy enough even with that.'

Had Danny invested a lot of time in his acts in the show? There had been some press reports that other contestants felt their coaches weren't giving them enough attention.

'He did, he definitely did. I think Will got a bit of criticism in the previous series for not being around as much – his profile is so global – but this year I found that any of the contestants I spoke to, no matter what team they were on, found that for their particular needs, each coach seemed to be able to give them the right advice. You got a lot of time with them – I think maybe a lot more than people would anticipate. You're not 24/7 with your coach – it is quite structured – but you can keep in contact outside of the programme. And Danny, definitely for me, would have given me plenty of time and made himself available on the phone.

'He would ring out of the blue with an idea, especially during the live shows. He would have rang me up and said, "Look ..." There were a couple of instances where I came down and met him at one of the studios he was working in in London because we were struggling to come up with a song choice for that week and he suddenly had a brainwave. And I went in and spoke to him and the two of us worked on it – that won't work, this one works. There were moments of sitting midweek having a bit of a crisis going: "Uh-oh, is this song going to work?"

'He would involve his band-mates and he would ring other people up as well. Because the thing about it is, sometimes the more people you ask, the more people you take advice from, especially when you're picking songs.

You'd be surprised at how limited the choices of songs are. Obviously you don't want to sing something that isn't suitable for your voice, and you don't want to sing something that people are fed up hearing. You want something people know but maybe haven't heard in a while, perhaps put a new twist on it.

'So song choice was critical and very difficult sometimes because you have to tick all those boxes. So Danny would definitely – always as soon as the quarter-finals and semi-finals were over – he was like: "Right, I'm going to have to start thinking about the next song." This was literally as soon as it was done and the announcement was made that I was getting through. He definitely thought very closely about things like that and, as I say, would have gotten people involved, whether that be Glen and Mark from the band or some of his other music friends.'

Had Andrea felt an immediate connection between them because they are both Irish?

'It probably helped, you know, in the sense that we would have been on the same page in terms of the humour and things like that. There was definitely that element of the Irish connection too. I remember him saying to me at the start, when he was trying to persuade me to go to him and not Tom, he was like: "You should always pick me because I'm Irish." And I was like, "Oh no, not the Irish card!" It was quite funny, but I think that did mean the two of us were on the same wavelength.'

Nikki Hayes is a popular radio DJ in Ireland with Spin

1038, having previously spent seven years with national broadcaster RTE on their 2fm station. 'The Script are very popular on Spin,' she says, 'absolutely. And it's not just the fact that they've got great music that tops the charts. I think Danny himself is a big factor. An awful lot of groupies would constantly be texting in looking for The Script to be played because of him alone, and we get them requested a lot!'

Nikki says that what impressed her about Danny when she has met him is that he has no rock-star ego and is always at pains to include the other band members at every stage. 'I've interviewed Danny a good few times. I've interviewed the band and him alone, especially when I was on RTE. I interviewed him in a Winnebago outside the Westbury Hotel in Dublin – I think it was for the launch of Oxegen – and also at HMV on Grafton Street and every time they were lovely.

'What I always love about Danny is that, as much as he is the frontman – and when a lot of people think The Script they think Danny – he doesn't think it's all about him. He always includes the lads. He never does the old "I'm the band" or anything like that; it's always about the other lads. Even if interviewers focus in on him, he always pulls the lads in on interviews as well.'

I asked Nikki if she thought that, by this stage in their career, are The Script here to stay?

'The one thing that makes them stand out and will give them longevity is that they know at the end of the day they are a band, and while Danny might have gone and done *The Voice* for a while, he has ultimately shelved that to concentrate on the band,' she says. 'So it's all about the music and they're down to earth. I know they are Dublin guys and Irish bands tend to be a little bit more down to earth than maybe some others, but they really are grounded. They remember people – they remember their fans, they remember interviewers. I guess it's a word you can overuse a lot, but they are just grounded and down to earth.

'My sister runs a bar over in Florida and The Script are one of the bands that would be played a lot there because they are so popular there and it's just nice to hear them when you are abroad as well.'

The secret of their success, Nikki believes, is that they are real, decent guys who wear their hearts on their sleeves and write meaningful lyrics. 'They sing about heartache, they talk about how they might have been out getting drunk,' she says. 'It's all very real, not airy-fairy rainbows and puppy dogs. It's real life that they sing about,' she says.

'They happen to be good-looking guys singing about it as well, which always helps! Plus they are extremely inoffensive. I don't know if that's a word that they would appreciate, but if you listen to The Script on the radio, you're not going to turn them off, because there is nothing about their music that makes you go, "Oh God, I can't be listening to that." In fact, it's the opposite – you just want to hear it more.

'The thing that makes them different from the likes of

U2 is that when you think about U2, obviously some of the guys like The Edge are great craic, but Bono was very much this untouchable figure on a pedestal above everybody else. The Script, Danny included, are very accessible. They are very much like the boy next door or your brother or your cousin – somebody that you feel like if you met them, you could go for a pint with them. I'm very sure that if you approached Danny on the street, he probably would stop and have a chat and say, "Hey, thanks for coming along." Whereas I'm not too sure Bono would reciprocate in the same way.

'Because they put the music out there first and the people followed afterwards, they don't have that egotistical "we're bigger than the music" approach. They're very much a band that realise their music is what they are and who they are personally comes after that. I think that definitely filters down through to the fans, to the media – the fact that people feel that they are someone they could know, they are someone nice, they are chatty and friendly.

'I think they'll be around as long as they want to be around, then after that their music will go on for a lot longer. As long as the boys want to be around people, people will want them to be around.

'That's just because of who they are as a whole package. The music is great, the guys are great, Danny's a great frontman – there's not one thing that I could actually say bad about them. That's coming from somebody who works in an industry that is saturated with bands, but they definitely stick out as one that you can definitely say: "Yeah, in 10, 20, 30 years' time, if the boys want to be around, they'll be around." They really worked their asses off for it, and they help other bands too, so as long as they keep that mindset, it leads to them being around for as long as they want to be.'

Boyzone singer Shane Lynch says that, as a fellow singer, he is full of admiration for the hard work Danny has put into his career and how that paid off. 'He's a good lad, he's done a great job,' he says. 'From back in the day he's always been pushing hard to become what he is today – he's worked hard at it.

'I admire the man. From the beginning he was always there, always trying different bands and different music projects and eventually he's made it – you stick at it and you achieve. Without a shadow of a doubt you can only respect the man for sticking at it, and he's a good, grounded lad who has done well, so fair play to him.'

Connor Phillips is an award-winning radio and TV presenter who co-hosts Cool FM's breakfast show and has worked for MTV and RTE in the past. He remembers being impressed by Danny from the first time he saw him live.

'We did a gig in the Limelight in Belfast, and they had only really one good single release,' he says. 'And then "The Man Who Can't Be Moved" came out – it was the one that caught everyone's attention. It had literally just been released and they were doing this corporate gig for us, a guest-only thing, and even then we knew there was something a wee bit different about them, and there was something a bit different about him as well.

'We get a lot of bands thrown at us as you would suspect, and you do encounter 15-20 bands you think are going to do very well and maybe don't. But there was something about that night – I remember I was right up at the front with the recording equipment and being moved out of the way by security and starting to get an idea of the pandemonium and the feeling that this is actually something a wee bit different here.

'It turned out they weren't doing any interviews because they were on a tight schedule. But I enjoy a good blag and I had the recording equipment as I was taking some audios so I could put a package together for the next day on air. Luckily enough one of the security guards recognised me, so I just rocked on in and I think the lads were a wee bit surprised to see me, as Mark was walking about in the nip, not a stitch of clothes on him.

'I just said, "Lads, can I get two minutes with you?" and they said "Yeah" and I just had a bit of craic with them. I had a good old natter with Danny and that was the first time I'd ever encountered him. First thing you go is, "Jesus, you're tall!" I'm 5ft 10in and he's towering above me, but it's strange: he's the nicest man you could meet – a really nice guy.

'And the thing you get about him is, he knows that this could all be over at any minute. He knows he's only a couple of bad album sales or a bad headline away from not being here any more. He's been around it over and over again; he knows he has struck gold and that makes him so easy to talk to.

'I interviewed Glen when they played the Odyssey in Belfast, and they have it down to a T. They know that this is exactly what they have been working for, for a decade if not more. They take care of their product, they take care of this thing that they have, the entity, and I tell you what – it's a flipping good entity.'

Connor knows very well how popular The Script are at his station from the amount of requests they get to spin their records, and says that he is a fan himself. 'It's very radio friendly and it's very easy for me as someone in commercial radio to get behind it. People could say, "He works in a commercial radio station – he has to say he likes it" but I'm not that type of presenter. If I don't like something I'll always be honest and say so, sometimes to my detriment.

'But I have to say, I like The Script, because their music is so radio-friendly, it's commercially very friendly. Granted, there is a little element of cheese about it. You look at a song like "Breakeven" – we've all, every single one of us, been through the whole break-up thing. You could say that's too obvious or too cheesy, but sometimes that's what works.

'When I was working in Dublin at RTE, the way Northern Irish people would get about Snow Patrol, was the way they felt about The Script – they were protective of them as a Dublin-based band and an Irish band.'

Connor believes the band will have longevity if they

keep working hard to establish themselves in America, and says that success there – as well as the boost they got to their career with Danny's stint on *The Voice* – is deserved after the years of graft they put in.

'For someone like Danny, he deserves his run of good luck after being battling at it for 10 or 15 years. Don't get me wrong: the first album went number one twice, their second album had gone number one – they had three number one albums and only released two albums! They were ridiculously successful from the point of view of an Irish rock-pop band. But then he gets the opportunity to go on *The Voice*, and in fairness to him he didn't do himself any harm and people warmed to him because of it. His personality – yeah, he's a wee bit quirky, he's a wee bit kooky, but people like that.

'I've interviewed them a few times and they are very overt with the attitude that this could be gone tomorrow. They're not going to do the whole "big I am" thing as they know it's going to work in their favour if they stay humble and true to their roots.'

CHAPTER 17

DANNY, CHAMPION OF THE WORLD

With more than a million followers for Danny personally on Twitter, five million likes for The Script on Facebook and a hundred million views on YouTube, you can see why Danny calls his fans 'The Script Family'. It's a two-way relationship – their fans love them, and Danny in particular – and they share the love back.

Danny admits to being particularly touched when fans go to the lengths of showing their commitment to the band by having Script-related inkings on their body. Come the summer of 2013, he made an appeal on Twitter for 'fans with tattoos of our name/lyrics etc' to send him pictures as he was 'starting a collection of them. Can't wait to see!'

Danny had won *The Voice* but it was time to bow out

and dedicate himself again to the band and their army of fans. The band were ready to get back on the road for the rest of the festival circuit, with thoughts already on album number four. They had sold more than five million copies in total of the three albums they had released since 2008 – an average of one million a year – but there would be an added significance to their new one, due to be released in 2014. It would be the last of their four-album deal with Sony Music, leaving them free to negotiate a new deal worth millions.

Danny's reason for quitting *The Voice*, after Jessie J had done likewise, was that he had recording commitments with The Script. 'I had two wonderful seasons on *The Voice* and as everybody knows, I gave it my heart and soul and couldn't be more proud of the show and what we have achieved,' he said in a statement. 'My focus will be on The Script moving forward, as we are about to embark on the most important part of our career as a band.'

Mark Linsey, BBC Controller, Entertainment Commissioning, said: 'Danny has been an absolute star – and a winner – on *The Voice* but we understand that he, like Jessie, has to focus on his music career and The Script have such an incredibly busy year ahead.

'*The Voice* coaches are all current music stars with recording and touring careers to manage alongside the show and we know this can be difficult to juggle. We are very sorry to see Danny go but wish him and the band the very best and hope they will come back and perform for us next series.'

Throughout the last series there had been strong rumours that the band had become frustrated by Danny's involvement with the show, in spite of the huge boost it was giving the band's profile. Part of the problem, it was said, was that *The Voice* took up so much of his time that The Script couldn't take advantage of all the extra publicity Danny was bringing them, and they had had to turn down dozens of lucrative gigs.

However, the band had made a joint decision that Danny should accept the invitation to go on *The Voice* in the first place – and that they would split his fee between them.

'Yes, we share everything we do,' they chorus in unison when I asked about it. But wasn't that a bit harsh on Danny? After all, he was the one doing most of the coaching work and having to perform for the cameras. Not at all, he insists – it's just good business. 'While I'm doing that, they are doing other things,' he points out.

The Voice has not only done wonders for The Script's profile, it has turned Danny into a household name. 'We brought ourselves to a much wider audience by me doing the show,' he agrees. 'Anybody watching it knows it's about music – and they know we're about music – so I think we did ourselves justice by me going on it. The power of getting involved in a Saturday night TV show is outrageous.'

Danny was also 'dating a special someone' again in the summer of 2013, breaking millions of hearts as he admitted the news, but whether or not she would prove to be as special as Irma, his longest relationship at four years, remains to be seen.

So it was back to business as The Script went on tour, knowing that Danny was done with his days as a TV talent show coach. And in some ways, returning to his rock star roots as an all-conquering hero meant that things could hardly have gone any better – increased profiles for him and the band, increased record and tour sales, the networking and contacts made – not least with co-star will.i.am, netting another No 1 song – and he had gone out on a high, winning with Andrea Begley. There was barely a negative worth talking about, but the time was right to get back to the band and concentrate on their music.

Just before show time Danny and his band-mates have their 'Cheeky Cheers' ritual in their dressing room – vodka and cranberry juice is Dutch courage for Danny and Mark, but teetoal Glen sticks to ginger ale. It's not their only ritual. The band like a full hour to themselves before they go on stage so that they are warmed up properly and ready to hit the ground running for an explosive and energetic performance. They never eat before a show either, which leaves them ravenous after, and they never talk about how a show has gone until the cold light of next day at the earliest.

'It's the wrong time after we come off stage,' says Danny. 'Emotions are so high. Before I go on, I pace the hallways like a caged tiger.'

On their last tour, they also added a fun element –

again cleverly thinking of their brand and having their business heads on – by finding a local angle everywhere they went that would please the fans. In Brighton their roadies were sent out and to buy beach-themed items such as beach balls and deck chairs, while in Cardiff it was masks bearing the face of Danny's co-star on *The Voice*, Tom Jones. And when the bizarre range of props are fired out to the crowd during the show, the band capitalise on it by taking pictures and posting them online on Facebook and Twitter to get fans talking.

All three band members would continue to be based in suburban West London (Danny is part of the London Irish crew that includes One Direction's Niall Horan and presenters Laura Whitmore and Amanda Byram) and – business savvy as ever with Mark controlling the purse strings – they continue to reinvest in the band. Each tour will be improved so that the fans keep having bigger and better experiences. Each album will be expertly produced to the standard fans have come to expect and appreciate, and each member would also have other interests, such as their own record and music publishing company. They also continue to work with other artists on writing songs – and they even penned songs as an audio companion piece for the young adult novel *Rock 'n' Roll Diaries*.

On tour, the band keep busy during the day by writing and recording in a portable studio equipped with its own soundproof audio booth. They even had a mini-recording studio put on their tour bus in America during the summer so that they could use the long hours travelling coast to coast over five weeks wisely, as well as help to pass the time.

It is in America that The Script know more work has to be done. They have enjoyed some success there, particularly with 'Breakeven' and 'Hall of Fame', but nothing near the heights they have hit in the UK and Ireland, Europe and Australia.

There can't be any rock band as well organised or forward thinking as The Script, and it's that discipline that should ensure they will continue to be successful for years to come. Mark is the driving force behind all this, as Danny told the *Sunday World* in July 2013.

'Right now we're sitting on a big piece of pie thanks to Mark. We're a better band because of Mark, who always said, "Business is a bigger word than music, we need to keep an eye on stuff. The more control we have, the less streams of revenue will be taken away from us." From the very start we paid ourselves a small wage and put the money in the bank. Unfortunately a lot of bands blow their advance money and burn out. Plus, we weren't paying other people a 20 per cent cut to do stuff because we were doing it ourselves. I was all about the music, so we were lucky that we had Mark keeping an eye on things.'

To use an analogy of his beloved Manchester United, Danny is the Eric Cantona to Mark's Sir Alex Ferguson. Danny steals the limelight as the glamorous and flamboyant frontman and the voice of The Script – he receives most of the glory, headlines and adulation. But

Mark is the planner, the organiser and the brains behind the scenes, as Danny himself admits: 'If it was left to me, I'd be sitting in the corner waiting to be discovered.'

But discovered he certainly has been – and boy, has he worked hard for it. Danny had had starry-eyed dreams of being a singer in a band since his teens, as he and Mark knocked about in that shed in Dublin. They never gave up on those dreams, despite the tough times. They didn't give up when Mytown didn't work out. Years of grafting in the US trying to get their foot in the door saw them start off making tea, but ending up writing songs for some of the biggest names in the music industry. They were so broke they had to steal ice to keep their food chilled in a bath because they had no money to run a fridge.

Now they are worth millions, but it is justice for all the work and effort they put in. They can say they earned it, and they are smart with it too. Level-headed rock stars do exist!

Does Danny have any regrets? Only that his dear dad Shay wasn't around to see the full extent of his success but, as always, Danny was able to deal with that regret by articulating it in song with 'If You Could See Me Now'.

If Shay can see him now, if he is looking down on him, he will be so proud of his boy – through grit and determination, hard work and skill, Danny has become a household name. From tea-boy to TV star with *The Voice*, his career has gone supersonic in the past five years since he and his band exploded on to the music scene proper.

Pin-up Danny is loved by millions and The Script's music is loved by millions more. Here's to the next chapter, for Danny and The Script.